Published by Ideasun Ltd
Spike Lodge, The Street, East Preston,
LITTLEHAMPTON, West Sussex, BN16 1JL
United Kingdom of Great Britain

Ideasun Limited.
Reg. No. 4021004
Registered office:
Martlet House, Unit E1, Yeoman Gate, Yeoman Way,
Worthing, BN13 3QZ, United Kingdom of Great Britain

HOW TO RAISE YOUR CHILDREN BIOLOGICALLY

Empathic Parenting: The counter-intuitive parenting technique for tots to teens.

Facebook group: totstoteens

www.totstoteens.org

ACKNOWLEDGEMENTS

I'd like to thank all the children who have been in my life, most particularly my delightful sons and daughters, without them I would have learned nothing and would have nothing to say.

I'd also like to thank Pietro Lantrua whose whimsical cartoons really caught the desired mood of the book, Deirdre Carolin for her great cover drawing and Carolyn Walton for her scrupulous proof reading and kind remarks.

Foreword

"Biological Parenting, what is that?" was my first thought when I saw the title of John Richards' book!

Is this a new parenting paradigm that had somehow cleverly sneaked past without my noticing? A newly coined parenting style based on physical anthropology? Which, by the way, I know absolutely nothing about - being a cultural, not a physical, anthropologist.

The first mental picture that came to mind after reading the words 'How to Raise Your Children Biologically' was that of biological forensic anthropologist Dr. Temperance "Bones" Brennan (played by Emily Deschanel) from the American TV series "Bones" ... and if you know her, she is probably not your first association to motherhood or parenthood!

So as you can imagine, I was intrigued! I love mysteries!

Not only was I curious as to what this book was about but also as to why John Richards chose me, a stranger from Denmark, for the great honour of writing the foreword of his book. Granted, I'm a mother and I own a fairly well visited parenting website, but still?

Well, it all started with a lovely email from John that he titled "We are Kindred Spirits!", in which he basically tells me that my way of thinking and writing resonates very well with him. And as our communication grew it became clear that John and I *do* have quite a lot in common - both in terms of our personalities and in terms of how we view the world.

Like me, John is a jack-of-all-trades kind of person - an optimistic, playful and curious 'multipotentialite', who loves new ideas and projects and who is also a bit of a science nerd. In my world calling someone a nerd is a compliment! :-)

Also, and more to the point in this context, we both share the big goal of wanting to make the world a better place for as many people as possible.

How?

Well, by sharing who we are, what we do and how we do it, hoping that it will benefit and help others.

I know that John has the ambition of doing that in many different fields, but in this case he wants to help parents and children create a better everyday life for themselves. He told me that as a former teacher he has seen some pretty heartbreaking examples of bad parenting that have prompted him to want to make a difference in the parenting field.

John simply wants to help parents and children grow. First and foremost grow from their hearts, well aided by their critical brain.

When you read this book, you will see that John is a bit of a norm rebel carrying the torch of science and reason in one hand but still being guided overall by the love and warmth coming from his big heart.

John is a man who has decided, "I want to do good, I want to help!" He wants to empower parents to start thinking critically about their own parenting style. I can just imagine John saying in the kindest non-patronizing tone of voice, "Parents, please stop; please take a moment to FEEL and to THINK ... does what you do make sense and make everybody happy?"

So back to the mysterious title, 'How to Raise Your Children Biologically' ...

Fortunately my curiosity was satisfied very early in the book. John's argument is really amazingly simple. In many ways we are like animals, he claims. And his logical argument is that if we are like animals, we can learn from them. If in our parenting we take as our point of departure 'what indisputably IS' and 'work WITH it', work WITH the nature of it, things become a lot easier and everybody becomes a lot happier.

For instance, one of his core arguments is that kids are born with natural empathy - so why not cultivate and enhance it? Learn to read your child's signals and go WITH them, fulfil their needs (which are not necessarily their 'wants' though).

If you don't, then you'll be swimming against the current and, as you know, that is hard and exhausting work ... plus you'll get wet and cold. You'll simply be working against nature, and nature will fight back in order to regain balance. That is nature's nature! That is your kid's nature. It will become a fight; a fight that everybody will lose. Follow your children's natural rhythms and fulfil their most natural needs. Go with the flow. Work WITH - not against!

Even though John is a former teacher and something of a walking encyclopaedia, he does not live in an academic ivory tower, far from it. He really masters the art of simple communication. He conveys his knowledge in a highly entertaining, involving and easy-to-read manner. He has a very clear and logical cause-and-effect-brain, which makes his arguments very easy to follow and understand.

Also he has a way of drawing you into his book with his personal and entertaining parenting tales, going all the way from his childhood in poor post-war Britain up to his own parenting life today. After reading this book, I really feel I've gotten to know John quite well.

One of the things I really like about John's personal tales is how he explains his interactions with his kids. He is really inventive and freely uses all of the repertoires of his body and brain. He really doesn't seem to care that he might look like a complete moron to an outsider, which I find very liberating. When he's with his kids, he's completely on their level - with an adult's mindset and big perspective, however.

Also to my joy, he is riding one my own hobbyhorses, showing how we parents are unconsciously determining the state of being of our children. That no matter what we do - whether we want to or not - we are teaching our children. ALL THE TIME, NON-STOP. Our sense of presence, the type of 'energy' we emit, the tone of our voice, how we handle challenges ... will be unconsciously taught to our children. Good stuff as well as bad. Why?

Well it's in kids' biology, he argues. Children ape! It's as simple as that. So why not use this fact as an advantage and in the book you'll get many examples of how to do just that.

Voilà, I hereby declare my own mission of discovering the meaning of 'biological parenting' to be accomplished. I hope it will have inspired you and that you're eager to get going with reading 'How to Raise Your Children Biologically'.

So please, sit down, lean back and enjoy this unique cocktail of well-researched scientific facts, heart-based parenting advice, entertaining personal tales spiced up with warm, yet dry, British wit.

Birgitte Coste
Owner of www.positive-parenting-ally.com
Anthropologist, mother and parenting guide
Copenhagen, Denmark

CONTENTS

INTRODUCTION

WHY HAVE I WRITTEN THIS BOOK?

Raising children is difficult; only a fool would say it is easy. Many books have been written on the subject, some good and some not so good. Probably the most notorious is a book called, 'To Train Up a Child'. The authors, American evangelists Michael and Debi Pearl, claim to have based it on Biblical sources. Several cases of child abuse have been brought against those who followed the writers' advice to whip three year olds until they are 'totally broken'! Sadly, some children have died as a result.

For a couple of years, during a varied career in education spanning almost half a century, I was Head of Science at a residential school for children with emotional and behavioural difficulties. The pupils' behaviour displayed evidence of unusual practices at home. Unfortunately, many of them ended up homeless, addicted or in jail soon after they left the care of the school.

The above are extreme examples, but less than perfect parenting continues to exist. When children grow up to have kids themselves, they look back to their own childhood for a model of how to rear them and any treatment they experienced gets passed down the generations. There is much room for improvement; this book is my contribution.

I'm a retired Science teacher who has taught thousands of children and young adults of all abilities from age 8 to 23, and I'm a parent twice over. I have two sons who are now married and producing grandchildren: three so far. Following the untimely death of their mother I remarried and now have two infant daughters.

So, as far as parenting is concerned, I'm an experienced practitioner. I have lived and worked with children all my life; there is not much that a child can do that I haven't seen before and have worked out a good way to respond to! Please don't expect me to be perfect; I want to stress that, like you, I am human and I make mistakes.

HOW COULD I WRITE THIS BOOK?

I know why you ask! The first time around, like most parents trying to juggle earning a living with raising children, it was difficult enough just coping – life was frantic.

Now, I'm that strange thing, a pensioner privileged to have a young family and I have the luxury of time to consider which parenting strategies might work best, and to write about them. This book is the result. I hope you find it helpful and enjoy reading it.

"Trying to juggle earning a living with raising children"

WHY 'HOW TO RAISE YOUR CHILDREN _BIOLOGICALLY'_?

In my career as a Science teacher, the subject I taught most was Biology and it became obvious to me that, since humans are animals, some of our growing Scientific knowledge of animal behaviour can be transferred to help the understanding, and improve the relationships, between human parents and their offspring. I came to the conclusion that parenting should be about enhancing the natural social empathy that our children are born with.

WHAT DOES THIS BOOK COVER?

Most developed countries provide plenty of help for the newborn, so this book concentrates on the period of childhood from toddler to pre-teen. I assume that you will feed your child when he or she is hungry and look after their other practical needs, so this book's main focus is on the relationship side of parenting, not on taking care of children or on teaching; I'm assuming that your children will go to pre-school and 'big' school for their education.

It may be helpful to say what this book is _not_ about – it doesn't deal with sexuality, it's not a parenting programme, nor a magic bullet. It's more like a target of a parenting style to aspire to and, like Olympic records, for most of us it is beyond reach!

I'm a teacher not a preacher so I'll try not to *tell* you what to do just, hopefully, help you to make your own decisions. Sadly, I frequently fail to take my own advice!

KEYPOINT:

Parenting should be about enhancing the natural empathy that our children are born with.

"The way kids learn to make good decisions is by making decisions not by following directions"
Alfie Kohn
(Unconditional Parenting)

PART ONE: *THE BIOLOGY*

WE ARE ANIMALS

The tradition of regarding mankind as separate from the animals is, quite simply, wrong.

It is a notion fostered in the scriptures; God gives us 'dominion over the animals' (Genesis 1:28 and 9:1-2, and in the Qur'an Majeed 35:38). For centuries most folks have interpreted the holy texts as permission to abuse animals in any way they like. All sorts of atrocities have been committed under that remit from putting a lion and a bear into a pen and seeing which wins the fight (the bear!), to factory farming.

We can now put animals into a rough ranking of brainpower. The Great Apes and the Cetaceans (dolphins and whales) have an awareness of self and live in complex societies like us. Going down the scale we come to the Corvids (crows), which can use tools and solve problems. Next are the social carnivores like Hyenas that can organize themselves into hunting groups to kill the much larger Zebra, then we have the herd animals (e.g. Cows) that have limited intellect and, below them, the Gastropods (Slugs and Snails) which probably lack consciousness.

"We can now put animals into a rough ranking of brainpower"

Recent evidence shows that domesticated animals such as sheep feel pain, express emotions, communicate between themselves and can recognize faces and voices. Dog owners will not be surprised by any of this. In acknowledgement of these facts, animal rights organizations are now improving the treatment of animals and some parts of Spain are even banning bullfighting!

Kanzi, a Bonobo chimpanzee (Pan paniscus) in Yerkes field station at Emory University in Georgia, USA, has a vocabulary of at least 384 words. By pointing to colourful symbols, he can build sentences, conjugate verbs and use different tenses. When he first ate kale he named it 'slow lettuce' because it takes longer to chew! He can order a pizza by pointing to the glyphs for 'bread', 'cheese' and 'tomato' - he is obviously a close relative of Homer Simpson!

"Deliver please"

Kanzi has continued to ape his handlers and can now gather wood, light a fire and barbecue his own food!

http://www.telegraph.co.uk/news/picturegalleries/howaboutthat/8985122/Amazing-photos-of-Kanzi-the-bonobo-lighting-a-fire-and-cooking-a-meal.html?image=6

Animals play. They have fun. Geese fly upside down! Dolphins surf in a ship's bow wave! There are no practical reasons for them to do these things. They just enjoy playing, like we do.

Since the advent of DNA sequencing we have discovered that humans (Homo sapiens) and the common chimpanzee (Pan troglodytes) share about 98.5% of their DNA!

The human species is not special! We can trace a continuum of gifted ancestor species back down the 'Tree of Life'. Man is just the current outcome of one direction of evolution, that of increasing intellectual complexity, because under many environmental pressures, such complexity can make an organism more fit to survive.

KEYPOINT:

Once you accept that we are animals, you open the door to *learning from animals.*

WE ARE *SOCIAL* ANIMALS

Humans are mammals, that is to say we are warm, hairy animals that give birth to live young rather than laying eggs. Most mammals (and birds) are, to a greater or lesser extent, social animals. Social animals live in communities larger than their immediate family. They have a level of organization that goes beyond the mother/offspring bond, with permanent groups of adults and youngsters living together throughout their lives. A social group exhibits special behaviour such as defending territory and establishing social dominance – a pecking order.

The largest mammalian social groups are called herds or flocks. These are made up of grazing mammals such as

25

Zebra and Wildebeest and sometimes hundreds move together in a swarm or stampede. The large herd size is based on the 'safety in numbers' principle. Females can give birth in the security of the centre of the herd. Predators may kill one or two weak individuals on the outside while the, fitter, majority escape. This is selection of the fittest in action.

Carnivore pack size is not so large, consisting of up to about twenty animals. Hyenas use a small group of co-operating hunters to bring down much larger prey such as Wildebeest. Our own nearest relatives, the apes, tend to form even smaller groups – from five to ten individuals, like an extended family.

Humans show strong signs of social dominance; we are the most hierarchical animals on planet Earth. Any group we form has to have a leader and followers. Military services are the most obvious example, with their complicated ranking systems from privates to Generals and Field Marshals, but hierarchies are evident in schools, hospitals, commercial companies, political parties, religious organizations, in fact, any field of endeavour.

Human pecking orders are more flexible than is the case in other animal societies. In civilized communities it is not just the oldest, largest, strongest individual who leads in everything, although this *was* true back in history when the warlord was simply the one with the biggest muscles, or who had a gun. Nowadays, we are usually more prepared to accept that some of us have skills suitable for certain tasks and, on other occasions, someone else should lead. This is the collegiate approach to organizing.

We also show territoriality, which reveals itself even in young children; they develop possessiveness about their territory as soon as they can voice the words, *'This is my home, my Dad, my computer.'* It can lead to territorial disputes.

Most human societies include 'domesticated' animals such as cattle and pets. Dogs have been bred from wolves. Humans have domesticated many wild animals, producing tame individuals with softer appearances and more docile temperaments.

A new study suggests that one of our primate cousins, the African ape known as the Bonobo chimpanzee (Pan paniscus), may have domesticated *itself* without human involvement! Anthropologist Brian Hare, of Duke University's Institute for Brain Sciences, noticed that the Bonobo looks like a domesticated version of its closest living relative, the common chimpanzee. The Bonobo is less aggressive than the chimp, with a smaller skull and shorter canine teeth and it spends more time playing and having sex. These traits are very similar to those that separate domesticated animals from their wild ancestors. They are all part of a constellation of characteristics known as the Domestication Syndrome. http://www.scientificamerican.com/article.cfm?id=tame-theory-did-bonobos

Humans have taken self-domestication to a new level – we

have civilized each other!

**Humans have taken self-domestication to a new level –
we have civilized each other!"**

*'Humans are a social species: we need each other to
survive. Civilisation is the end product of hundreds of
generations of people working together to achieve more than
what any of them could alone. Groups that behave nicely do
better than groups that squabble.'*
Luis Villazon, writing in BBC Focus magazine.

KEYPOINT:

Social animals such as humans have evolved to co-operate for their mutual benefit. We are born to be good to each other!

African saying, 'It takes a village to raise a child"

THE BIOLOGY OF BEHAVIOUR

Biologists recognize two types of behaviour: instinctive and learned behaviour.

Instinct is the *innate* behaviour of an animal; it's what they are born with. When a grizzly bear hibernates or your kitten purrs, they are performing instinctive behaviours.

"Night folks!"

A baby kangaroo, hardly more developed than a worm, will wriggle into its mother's pouch immediately it is born. Newly hatched sea turtles will automatically move down a beach towards the water. Other examples of instinctive behaviour include courtship dances, fighting for dominance, homing and the building of nests.

This way!

'Higher' animals, including humans, can also *learn* behaviours. Learning is often done by watching others who know how to do something that the watcher doesn't. Many different animals have been observed learning from their colleagues or even from other species! See more in the Teaching and Learning section.

Air, water, and food are metabolic requirements for survival in all animals, including humans, so meeting those fundamental needs is the first item on the agenda. Next on the list are shelter, sleep, friendship and sex. Satisfying these needs and desires drives most behaviour.

There is just one way in which humans *are* special; we are the only animals to wear clothes – personal transportable shelter, although some animals make 'shells' from locally available objects or cover themselves in camouflage or protective materials when they are vulnerable.

The habitat available to most animals is so vast that their range will be limited within it; most creatures, apart from whales and the arctic tern, which flies from pole to pole twice a year, simply can't travel the enormous distances available. Limitations can be either geographic or temporal.

An animal with a geographic limit is said to have a territory. That territory is the source of the animal's food and water so it will have to be defended. Some mammals mark their boundaries with their excreta. Any intruder who doesn't smell right will be treated to a threat display and may be attacked. Humans show this territorial behaviour in the ownership of properties surrounded by walls or fences and by loyalty to towns and countries.

"This is yours, that's mine."

Territorial behaviour even extends to close quarters – we are all conscious of our *intimate* space, a zone close enough for physical contact that we only let our family and lovers into. Going outwards is the 'personal space', with a radius of about 1.2 metres (4 feet), which we find acceptable for talking with friends but we feel uncomfortable when strangers come that close. Watch how people sit on a park bench to see this in action. Friends might cuddle up together while strangers will leave a gap between them.

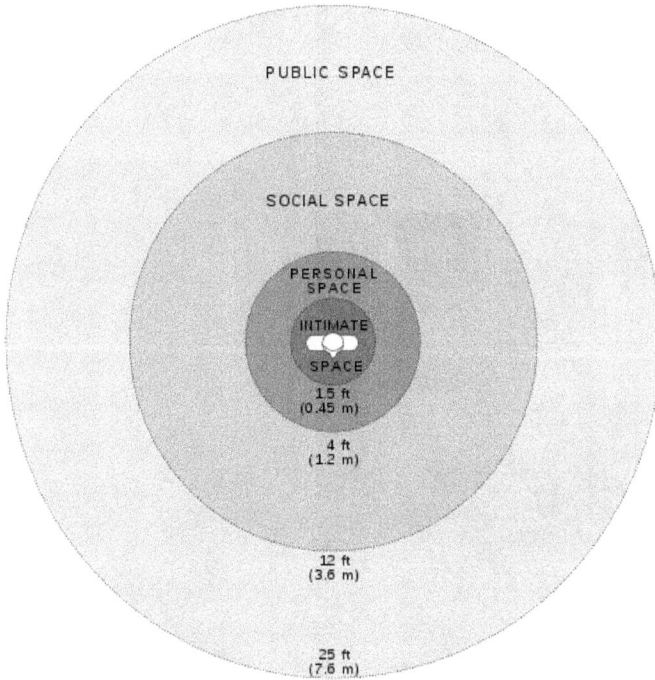

PUBLIC SPACE

SOCIAL SPACE

PERSONAL
SPACE

INTIMATE

SPACE

1.5 ft
(0.45 m)

4 ft
(1.2 m)

12 ft
(3.6 m)

25 ft
(7.6 m)

From Wikipedia Commons

It's sometimes useful to try to enforce 'personal space' distances between disagreeable siblings – see later in the section on Transport.

The other type, Temporal Separation, involves being active at different times of day. All animals have to accommodate the day/night cycle as the Earth revolves. Some, such as bats and moths, have evolved to be active at night but most take darkness as a cue to go to sleep. Parents would be well

35

advised to work with this tendency, not against it – see later in the Daily Routine section.

"Night-time, better get up!"

The daily cycle inflicts a routine on animals that extends to many physiological functions. We may find that our bowels habitually perform at a specific time of day – usually when we get up. Our tummies rumble at lunchtime to remind us to eat. My advice is to get children into a routine and to try to stick with it – see later in the Daily Routine section.

While the above applies to most creatures, *social* animals have another behavioural impetus: Hierarchy. They have to develop a 'Pecking Order'. Group stability is best maintained

if one member is the boss. Gorillas have a dominant male –
the oldest 'silver back'.

"I'm the boss, you're fired!"

We are all constantly monitoring each other's behaviour. The
signals you give off, even unconsciously in the form of body
language, affect the way you are perceived by your children.
If you behave as if ants terrify you, they will copy you. If you
constantly correct them, they will think life is all about conflict
and defiance.

It's such a responsibility being a parent - everything we do
has a consequence, every action has a reaction. Do you
want to set the right tone?

KEYPOINTS:

Social animals have instinctive behaviours (Nature) and can learn from each other (Nurture). It's best to work with the day/night cycle.

THEORY OF MIND

Maintaining a society requires co-operation. It's difficult to see how co-operation can be achieved without a 'Theory of Mind'. 'Higher' animals have evolved this ability.

'Theory of Mind' is the ability to recognize mental states such as desires, pretences, beliefs and knowledge in oneself, and to understand that others have beliefs, desires, knowledge and intentions that are different from one's own. Being able to attribute mental states to others and understanding them as causes of behaviour enables members of a group to co-ordinate their activities.

The precursors of a Theory of Mind include abilities such as attention, intention, recognizing that the image in a mirror is a refection of yourself and not another creature, and the understanding of false belief.

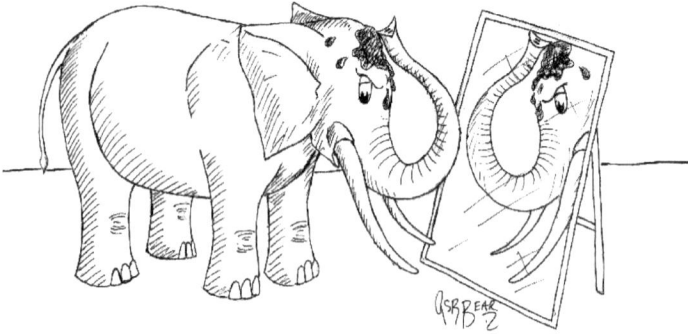

"Is that mud on my face?"

"Who are you?"

Tests to investigate false-belief are based on the following scenario: a child is shown two dolls, Sally and Anne, who have a basket and a box, respectively. Sally also has a marble, which the investigator places in her basket, and then Sally is taken away. While she is out, the investigator makes Anne take the marble from Sally's basket, putting it in her own box. Then Sally is returned, and the child is then asked, *"Where will Sally look for the marble?"*

The child passes the task if she answers that Sally will look in the basket, where Sally watched it being put, but fails the task if she answers that Sally will look in the box, where the child knows the marble has since been put, but doesn't realize that Sally cannot know it's now in there. Research using false-belief tasks has given fairly consistent results: normally-developing children are usually unable to pass the tasks until around the age of four, so the researchers think that a Theory of Mind develops in the fifth year.

I disagree. My eighteen-month-old daughter plays with me as though she understands what is in my mind. On one occasion, she sat on my favourite part of the sofa so I pretended not to see her and gently sat on her! She thought this was so funny that, now, when I leave my seat she rushes to sit there so we can repeat the joke! Another time, she was sat on the bed and I gently pushed her over backwards. Now

I only have to say 'push' and she does it herself just to amuse us! How can she join in these games without knowing that we have minds in our heads and being able to anticipate how we will react?

You may watch these skills develop in your baby. Shortly after birth their eyes begin to focus and they will start giving you their attention. Later, they develop a will of their own and you can begin to see their intentions such as, *"I want to climb on to the sofa"*

KEYPOINT:

Theory of Mind permits empathy, which appears to be an innate potential ability in humans, but one that requires social experience over many years to bring to ultimate fruition. That's where parents, grandparents, teachers and the wider community come into the picture; we have opportunities to nurture.

EMPATHY

If you have a Theory of Mind, you can relate to another individual's pain and joy. Sharing emotions is known as Empathy. Apes have been documented consoling each other after a conflict. Recent neuro-ethological studies of animal behaviour, suggest that rodents may exhibit empathic abilities because they emit ultrasonic chuckles of pleasure when playing together! Even baby ants have been observed playfully biting each other!

Empathy can be observed in communal yawning and body synchronization – one person crosses his legs and others subconsciously do the same. Emotional contagion occurs in situations of grief inspired by disaster. So empathy is the ability to recognize and understand the states of mind, including beliefs and desires and, particularly, the emotions of others. It is often characterized as being able to 'put oneself into another's shoes'.

Experiments show that there is a continuity of evolved morality between other primates and humans. Some monkeys and apes exhibit empathy and consolation, others show prosocial tendencies such as reciprocity and fairness.

45

See:

Humans have evolved an innate potential for empathy and we can be nurtured to conceptualize the feelings of other people. The small number of people who lack this ability are considered to be autistic and a very few of them may develop into sociopaths or psychopaths.

Understanding how others feel leads to behaviours that are socially acceptable. This means we have been selected by nature to learn to discipline ourselves to be nice to each other, within our own communities at least.

Scientists are now beginning to unravel the mechanism that drives our pro-social behaviour. According to one researcher, the main cause of good behaviour seems to be the hormone Oxytocin. Originally evolved to induce labour in mammals and influence the bond between mother and baby, it now appears its effects may extend to emotions related to other social behaviours. If an oxytocin-laced mixture is sprayed into your nose, you get the warm fuzzy glow associated with kindness and generosity. Chemically related drugs like Ecstasy give that 'loved up' feeling that makes us want to trust each other and have a hug. The *'oxytocin makes us moral'* hypothesis is taken with a pinch of salt by other scientists but, if you want to find out more read 'The New Science of what makes us Good or Evil' by Paul Zak. For the opposite view see: Ed Yong's article,

http://www.slate.com/articles/health_and_science/medical_examiner/2012/07/oxytocin_is_not_a_love_drug_don_t_give_it_to_kids_with_autism_.html

Psychologists from Sigmund Freud to Jean Piaget and Lawrence Kohl have argued that we begin life as amoral animals and social scientists have long considered babies to be born as 'blank slates'. Now an astonishing series of experiments is challenging this established view that our morality is entirely shaped by our parents and our experiences of society.

At the age of six months our babies can barely sit up - let alone crawl or talk but, according to Psychology Professor Paul Bloom of Yale University, they have already developed a moral code!

http://www.nytimes.com/2010/05/09/magazine/09babies-t.html?pagewanted=all&_r=0

The results of this recent research suggest that the difference between good and bad may be hardwired into the brain at birth. Obviously, later experiences, due to parenting among other things, may modify this innate sense of morality.

So basic morals and ethics are behavioural traits that have an inherited component. We have evolved basic morals and don't have to get them from venerable scriptures (writings). Some people have difficulty coming to terms with that.

Recent research shows that nicely behaved baboons live longer. This means that they will have more opportunity to reproduce and their personality traits will appear in more descendants until their socially acceptable behaviour predominates in the group.
http://news.sciencemag.org/sciencenow/2012/10/for-some-primates-survival-of
th.html?ref=hp&utm_source=buffer&buffer_share=32cdb#.U
GtT5VwvzPA.reddit

Yes, behaviour is, at least partly, inherited. That explains how we can breed dogs to perform certain functions; Terriers fearlessly go down holes after rats, rabbits and even foxes. Water Spaniels fetch ducks that their handler has shot down, even if they fell in a pond. Pointers adopt a posture directing a hunter towards his quarry. You would have your work cut out if you tried to train one specialised dog to do the job of another – imagine attempting to get a foxhound to work as a sheep dog!

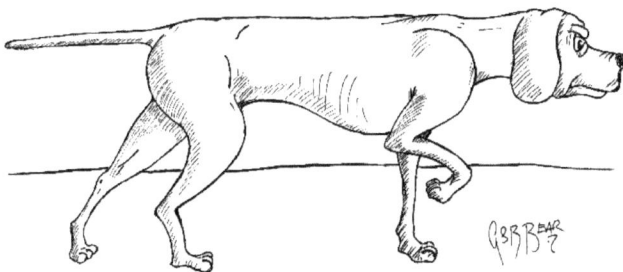

"See the duck? It's over there!"

The inheritability of behaviour also explains how monkeys can be observed driving a recalcitrant member out of their pack. They haven't read a religious tome to get their moral values!

We now know there is continuity from other primates to ourselves showing how morality has evolved. Various mammals, including elephants, have been shown to understand co-operation. Chimpanzees and Capuchin monkeys have pro-social tendencies including reciprocity, fairness and consolation.

So, if behaviour is partly inherited (due to nature) and the other part of the mix is due to upbringing (nurture), a good question would be, how big a part is the inherited component and how big the nurture contribution? Well, the truth is we really don't know, but it might be the same share out as is the case with intelligence. It's a contentious subject, but recent research indicates that intelligence may be between about fifty and seventy-five per-cent inherited. Since we don't have to teach terriers to go down holes, that proportion may also apply to behaviour.

Social animals have to behave acceptably within their group. In order to do this successfully they have to obey the behaviour codes of their own community and they probably have an up to seventy five per cent inherited propensity to learn to do that. That's a good beginning point for raising a child isn't it? Our children start out on our side!

KEYPOINT:

Our children want to fit in from the day they are born. If only we can work *with them* by encouraging acceptable behaviour and denigrating unacceptable behaviour, they should turn out to be good members of society.
Conversely, could it be that anti-social behaviour in adults is largely the result of bad parenting?

My favourite empathy related joke:

If you dislike someone, you should walk a mile in his shoes, because if you still don't like him then, at least you are a mile away, and you've got his shoes!

> *There are no bad dogs, only bad dog owners.*
> (A well-known saying in dog owning circles)

FAMILY SIZE

Dogs and pigs sometimes have a litter that is so large the last one is a weedy specimen called the 'runt'. Did you know that recent research suggests that human firstborns have a slightly longer life expectancy, on average, than subsequent children? It is not generally recognized how big an impact the number of children in a family can have on how they grow up and the persons they develop into.

In many Western countries, the welfare state safety net has meant that, since the Second World War, there has been no incentive to have large families solely for the purpose of providing for and looking after their parents when they get elderly. Our children do not have to be a substitute for a pension and free health care. Also, following the advent of the contraceptive pill in the 1960s, acceptable technologies for restricting family size have been available.

These developments are reflected in our own family histories – my parents (both born before the introduction of the UK welfare state) had five and six siblings (and one stillborn each) but their own generation stopped reproducing at one, two or three offspring. The data is also mirrored in national statistics – a couple should produce 2.2 children to ensure their own replacement and maintain a stable population size.

Today, in Italy for example, the current average family size is 1.8 children so that country's population would be contracting if it were not for immigration.

Reducing the number of humans is probably good in the long term, for both planet Earth and its residents, but the transition to lower numbers is causing difficulty. The makeup of society has been skewed with fewer people in the working period of life and more at the pensionable age. This has caused economic problems for governments.

China has tackled their enormous population growth in a different way. Being an authoritarian society it was deemed acceptable for the government to instigate a 'one child' policy with various sanctions. Unfortunately, since the Western style welfare safety net is lacking, parents preferred to make sure their one child was a boy who might work hard to support them in old age. Sadly, girl babies were killed at birth and the outcome, some twenty years on, is a swathe of frustrated and angry young men, lacking partners and causing trouble.

OK, I recognize that this book will not put the world to rights and that the size of your family may not be entirely under your control! If you do have intentions to limit it though, there follows some points you might like to consider.

HOW MANY CHILDREN?

Single children have had undeserved bad press. Since, in most societies, it is more common to have siblings, it is not surprising that having a brother or sister or two is thought to be the 'normal' state of affairs. The opposite side of this coin is that singletons are considered to be a bit odd. It all began 120 years ago when a pioneering child psychologist, Granville Stanley Hall, published "Of Peculiar and Exceptional Children" which described singletons as permanent misfits! Psychology was in its infancy and next to nothing was known about credible research practices. See: an article on page 36 in Time, July 19th 2010.

It's time to come clean: I am an only child myself, although I was raised in an extended family situation with cousins – the best of both worlds. Thanks to Granville Hall, individuals like me are commonly regarded to be spoilt, selfish and unable to share. The assumption is that parents have doted on them and lavished every available privilege onto each lock of their precious hair.

Well, that certainly wasn't my experience being raised as a child in the austere post-war Britain of the nineteen-fifties. I tell my children and grandchildren, as they demand the latest computer games, that all I had to play with at their age was a stick; and that's not far from the truth.

But, whatever the level of affluence, what parents of the 'lonely only' have *not* given their child is a resident playmate; they have to look outside the home for the companionship of other children. To understand how significant that might be in a child's formative years, I now want all you brothers and sisters who are reading this to try to imagine growing up with just your parents at home.

Being an only child often means you grow up less needy; you pretty much know you've got your parents' undivided attention. You have no one to compete with so, if you cry, you probably are really hurting not just 'taking a dive' like footballers or siblings trying to get noticed.

It's not necessarily a lonely existence, just one in which the child's main companions is his or her parents. Such children tend to be treated like little adults and expected to behave appropriately for adult society from an early age. They don't get talked down to and do get included in mature conversation, invited to join in with household decision-making and taken into confidences. What's wrong with that?

Now, imagine yourself transported into a household of brothers and sisters for a moment; if you're from a large family this will be easy for you. It's also easy for me because I have raised two boys and am now father to two girls whilst also observing my grandchildren's interactions.

With the exception of twins, which are a special case, a brother or sister will either be younger or older. This is a double-edged sword. It could be argued that having a child companion of approximately similar age is good from the point of view of sharing activities and development - having someone for playing with and growing up together.

In practice it's often different from that ideal notion because having playmates of unequal abilities due to small age differences leads to winner and loser scenarios. The older, bigger, more advanced child inevitably starts bragging about their successes and the junior one flounces off in tears. The potential for bullying arises right there.

The older child perceives their superiority and may start to impose their will on the younger one. Bossiness rears its ugly head. Scorn is poured. Each child becomes more inclined to impose reciprocal sanctions on their sibling, *"I'm not going to play with you anymore"*, *"Don't touch my things"*, *"Keep out of my toy cupboard"*, etc. That's the start of possessiveness and divisive territorialism.

BATTLE OF WILLS
Of course, many junior siblings are not willing simply to be

submissive. They may become grumpy and fight back. They may say, *"I hate you"*, with some justification and, when parents or other adults try to intervene, the hatred may be redirected at them. The sibling's friendship deteriorates until physical violence results and the imposition of adult authority becomes necessary. When unseen by parental eyes, their interaction can easily escalate into a physically abusive relationship. Is anyone recognizing this little drama? Many brothers feel the need to apologize for their childhood behaviour when they become men!

What if the youngest one feels they have to fight back harder because they have a size disadvantage? They might overcompensate by fighting 'dirtier'. Biting and kicking become legitimate tactics in their minds. Is this the start of the 'small man syndrome'? Are we observing a human version of the process that makes little dogs yappier than big dogs?

Both contenders know they are trapped in their association; no matter how appallingly they treat each other during the day, they are secure in the knowledge that they will share the same bedroom that night. That fact sort of normalizes, even 'legalizes', the relationship of one oppressive tyrant and one underling. Parents of siblings tend to think, *"Ah, that means they've cuddled and made-up."* But, what if it actually means that one of them had realized they've got a captive they can try out their best moves on, and the other one had accepted it's his or her destiny to be a victim before they both fell asleep exhausted? Severe sibling bullying can damage personality.

None of this can happen in the singleton's household. No sibling bossiness, no bullying, no need to develop possessiveness or territorial attitudes, no abusive relationship, no hatred or fighting and no wails of, *"He just did so-and-so to me!"* It's quite peaceful!

On the other hand, 'only' children have no automatic, unearned guarantee of constant companionship. A singleton is an observer of all the undesirable behaviour in others and soon learns that the best way to make friends with other children in the neighbourhood is actually to be nice to them! OK, singletons may be poor at fighting, and uninterested in having a 'roughhouse', but what's wrong with that?

Every school day I used to walk about a mile to the bus stop with our neighbour's son. I always had a sixpence and bought a little bar of chocolate, which I shared equally with this boy. We enjoyed the companionship of walking along and chatting together and to eat all the chocolate myself would have upset the relationship. He expressed surprise at my generosity; it was a new experience for him having been raised in the Sibling Contest Environment! I wasn't trying to buy his friendship, we weren't even in the same year at school; it just seemed the fair thing to do. Singletons grow up quickly, learn how friendship works, and soon tend to consider the squabbling behaviour they observe in siblings as a bit childish and unnecessary.

So I contend that the stereotypical image of an only child as a mean, self-centred brat is wrong. That is an unjustifiably negative assumption conferred by the widespread experience of living as young combatants in the aggressively contested world of siblings.

The reality is the very opposite. Singletons learn that friendship is not an automatic right resulting from growing up together but is a precious commodity that has to be earned and it depends on sharing, being fair and generally behaving considerately and tolerantly towards each other.

Family size is an important consideration in today's world. Parents need to bear in mind that two children are more than twice the work of one because while you are sorting out one, the other is creating more havoc!

The age gap is significant also – if one is more or less 'self catering' in terms of being able to dress, toilet and feed themselves while you deal with the nappies of the younger one, it reduces the work load. You may even get older ones to help.

For an older child, a young sibling can provide an object lesson in thinking about someone other than themselves. This is good empathy enhancement training. When the older child is trying to use the younger child as a dolly and the young one starts crying, you can say, *"She doesn't want you to do that, how would you feel if you had an older sister constantly trying to make you play the baby?"*

The other lesson that older siblings can learn from their interaction with a younger brother or sister is to do with setting an example. They soon notice that the younger child apes them - copies whatever they do. A parent can introduce the idea that big brother or sister has to be careful not to set a dangerous example, like climbing a tree, in front of the little one.

Tolerance can also be taught through these interactions. A parent can point out that when the older child was a baby, mum or dad watched baby TV with them and got their pleasure from watching their baby's pleasure. Now it's their turn to let their younger brother or sister watch the baby channel and to enjoy it through them. Isn't it good to have considerate siblings!

Sometimes though, the first one regresses when the second one arrives. They find they now have to compete for their parent's attention; they may suddenly feel less secure and want your help once more to do up buttons, use the toilet, etc.

As they grow, brothers and sisters are going to require separate bedrooms, so there is a house size and cost implication to take into account. Have you thought about the big car you are going to need?

Once there are three or more children, the parents are outnumbered so, unless one child is much older and can help with parenting, extra manpower may be required in the shape of an au pair, nanny or live-in granny.

If both parents are working there is, often costly, childcare provision to arrange. The pressure on parents reduces when children start going to school but we still have to cope with fulltime parenting for thirteen weeks of the year during school holidays, not to mention all the evenings and weekends. This is why mothers often have to accept low paid work in education to fit in with their children's term times.

Hopefully, responsible parents will take these factors into account – it is raising the next generation of humans that we are talking about here! I think there is nothing wrong with having a single child and my advice for larger families is to space them out with an age gap of about three years.

Another important consideration is how old a couple are when they become parents. The risk of genetic mutations arising in offspring correlates with age. A 40-year-old father is three times more likely to conceive a child that becomes schizophrenic than a 20-year-old father and twice as likely to conceive a child that develops autism. The incidence of a Downs Syndrome child increases from 1 in 1250 for a 25-year-old woman to 1 in 100 for one 40 years old.

http://www.webmd.com/baby/news/20090309/older-fathers-lower-iq-in-kids?page=2

I'm not cheeky enough to make a personal recommendation for you; I'm just trying to help you come to your own decisions! One final thing: do not expect any two children to be the same; even identical twins can be quite different in personality and behaviour!

KEYPOINT:

Choice of family size can have lasting implications – think carefully!

BREASTFEEDING

As stated earlier, the focus of this book is not on the first few months of life – I consider baby care to be well covered elsewhere. However, this section is an update on recent research on the subject of breast-feeding.

It's not surprising that 'Breast is Best' because the output of human mammary glands has evolved to be ideally tailored to the demands of our babies. The first food ('colostrums') a baby receives from its mother contains a dose of antibodies to tide the child over until its own immune system starts to function and, thereafter, her milk varies in composition to meet the changing needs of a developing human infant.

Cows milk has a very different makeup and calorific value and doesn't vary as the child grows. Proprietary baby milks are an attempt to mimic the real thing but mum's homebrew is still best by far. In the same way, cow's milk is perfect for calves!

What has just become known is that *how* a baby is fed is also important. Two 'feeding patterns' have been investigated: four hourly interval feeding and on-demand feeding. Ten thousand babies born in the early 1990s have been followed through life and those who were fed on-demand turn out to have higher IQs, as measured in SAT tests at school, than those fed at regular intervals!

Dr Maria Iacovou, from the **Institute for Social and Economic Research,** said: *"The difference between schedule and demand-fed children is found both in breastfed and in bottle-fed babies."*

The data was drawn from the Avon Longitudinal Study of Parents and Children. It involved researchers from Essex and Oxford Universities and was published in the European Journal of Public Health.

However, the researchers also concluded that mothers who fed their babies according to a schedule were more likely to get more sleep and more enjoyment out of parenting. Make your choice!

The other piece of 'conventional wisdom' that is now being challenged is the notion that breast-feeding should continue for six months. This may be good advice in developing countries where there have been some baby deaths through inappropriate early weaning but, in the developed world, it may be better to introduce new tastes earlier before the 'window of acceptance' for the introduction of innovative flavours closes.

'Attachment parenting' has recently hit the headlines. This is probably more because it gives magazines an opportunity to improve their sales figures by featuring a young mother breast-feeding her three-year-old son on the cover, than because it represents a radical advance in parenting. Once you have got over the journalistic shock tactics it turns out that so-called 'attachment parenting' is just about carrying your baby in a sling next to your body, sharing a bed with your young child and breast feeding as long as possible. Most of us are already 'attachment parents'!

KEYPOINT:

If you possibly can, breastfeed on demand!

CHILD CARE IN AND OUT OF YOUR HOME

Many animal mothers will look after the nest for their offspring – budgerigars pick up poo and throw it out, bitches eat their puppies' early excrement!

This morning, my one-year-old daughter managed to open the, allegedly, childproof cap to the bottle of infant paracetamol and spill the entire sticky contents on the study carpet! There is a lesson to be learned from incidents like this. We have to ask, is carpet the best floor covering for the rooms that toddlers go into? What is the best floor covering? Tiles or wooden flooring that can be swabbed like the decks of a pirate ship, that's what! We do have them elsewhere downstairs.

When you have toddlers, you will get spills and damage to the furniture. They will put their fingers in the butter! My eldest daughter has drawn on the walls and stuck things on the doors. I can't complain too much, when I was a toddler I made a hole in a lath and plaster wall with a screwdriver! We are resigned to waiting for them to grow up before redecorating. You may have put all the blue ornaments in the blue bedroom and look on with dismay as your toddler carries them around the house but what's important: your show home, or your family? (By the way, if you're prepared to

69

let your child's room get in a mess so they experience the frustration of not being able to find something when they want it, then you can teach tidiness!)

The toilet is a special place for children. When they are training to use it, a good trick is to turn the basin tap on to stimulate the flow of wee! You will have to rewind the toilet roll several times before they get fed up with pulling on it. I recommend squashing the roll so it rotates badly and doesn't deliver great lengths easily. *Elyptify* your toilet roll!

You know how women like to nag men about putting the toilet seat down after they have urinated? Well, I've always been assiduous about doing this and have been able to put the boot on the other foot by nagging my wife to put the lid down. After years of her failing to do this, it only took one occasion when a toddler dropped her watch down the toilet for her to learn the error of her ways!

The staircase is a particular hazard and should be gated top and bottom from the moment your child becomes mobile to the time they can negotiate the steps safely. You can help them learn to climb up by following behind as they put a knee on each step and you can help them learn to come down sitting on their bottoms. In the early stages of descending you can sit them on your lap as you bump down on your own bottom. They will love this – it's like a mini fairground ride. It will be a great relief though, when you can take the gates away!

Obviously, it is necessary to safeguard your children from the dangers of home; things like scissors, knives, toilet cleaner and the drinks cabinet. Many things can simply be put high up out of their reach while the children are small. There are plenty of devices for preventing access to cupboards – for example, if there are double doors you can just tie the knobs together. Do an Internet search for 'toddler proofing' and you will find plenty of advice. Here's a tip – always have a high shelf so you can put things up out of reach.

In most developed countries, childcare in specialized establishments – preschools and nurseries, is available from an early age. Check these out and go with the one that offers a rich environment to stimulate your child, which has a good staff to child ratio, and which gives a daily report on your child's experience, if possible.

Starting pre-school involves breaking the parent-child bond which can be painful at first with some crying (on both sides!) but, a good establishment can probably offer better opportunities than the average home and, meeting other children and having meals with them, helps greatly with socializing. Both of my daughters get to paint, glue, listen to stories and do dressing up far more often than they would at home. We even have fun on the way there – it's surprising how many times a buggy can 'accidentally' crash into things accompanied by much hilarity!

At one of our local pre-schools, the toddlers get sat on potties at nappy change time and, sometimes, the communal nature of the experience gets them to wee together! It's a bit like old latrines in men's toilets or the multi-holed toilet benches of the Ancient Romans! My Grammar School had a roofless building in the playground with a gutter for boys to pee into!

KEYPOINT:

Whether at home or school, it is important to ensure that your children get a safe and stimulating environment.

DAILY ROUTINE

Humans, like almost all animals, have a circadian rhythm (circa = about, dia = day); that is, our bodies recognize the daily changes caused by the earth's rotation on its axis and respond to them. If you've ever experienced jet lag you'll know what it feels like when your patterns are disrupted. Take a look at this excellent diagram from Wikipedia Commons:

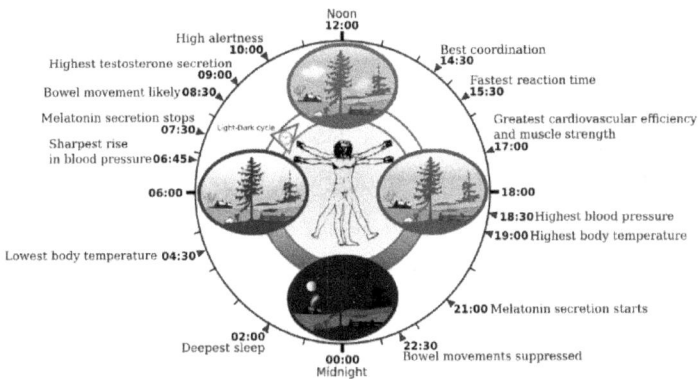

As you can see we are programmed to sleep when it is dark and to defaecate in the morning! Sports activities would be best done in the afternoon and sexual activities upon waking up! We have a body clock.

BEDTIME:

We all need our sleep; recent research suggests that's when the brain does its 'filing' of the day's events. Sleep

73

deprivation is a form of torture. Rats deprived of sleep die in 17 to 20 days!

Obviously it makes sense for parents to go with the flow rather than try to battle against nature. You can recognize tiredness by yawning, irritability and crying despite your children's inevitable attempts to deny it. Tired children also get more clumsy, whiney and accident-prone.

Put your children to bed at dusk! If it's not dark enough, simulate it by pulling the curtains. It's surprising how many parents imagine their children will easily fall asleep with the light on or the curtains pulled back. Don't try to resist natural tendencies! Yes, a child who is utterly exhausted will conk out eventually but at what cost? Being late to sleep tonight means grumpiness tomorrow morning. Why not take the easier route of a darkened room and a regular bedtime? We know this works with animals – we put a hood over the head of a hawk to keep them quiet until we want them to fly and, if we are transporting an animal like an Oryx we cover it with a blanket.

Sleeping with the light on means that, if he or she wakes up in the middle of the night, they will probably find it harder to drop off again. I recommend training them to welcome the warm enfolding friendliness of night and not to become prey to fear of the dark, which will only bite them back later in life when they are trying to sleep with others!

If you've ever kept a caged bird and let it fly free in a room, you will know that the way to get it back in its cage is to black out the room then you can just go over to it and pick it up. Escaped birds won't fly in the dark and if you want your budgie to stop bashing its bell during the TV news, just cover its cage with a cloth.

Don't forget, we are animals and will probably calm down in the dark like most other mammals and birds. Thanks to dusk being a slow process in the middle latitudes, parents can make bedtime about eight pm. If it's not dark enough, pull the curtains or blinds. Equatorial regions are a bit different with a short dusk and less attention being paid to the clock; it may be more about tiredness there.

Going through a sequence of events in preparation for bed sets the scene, which is a good idea. Stopping play, tidying up, bathing, cleaning the teeth, having a wee, getting into nightclothes and having a story to read. This routine will assist with gradually calming your child and helping them to slip into unconsciousness.

Some of the old techniques really do work. A babe in arms

really can be put to sleep by carrying him or her while walking up and down singing a lullaby. It helps if this is being done in a quiet, darkened room. Since we are tactile animals, it often helps to satisfy the sense of touch. A child who has recently been weaned may miss the feeling of the breast so give them something else to fondle! Some children go for a piece of silky, satiny fabric while others may become attached to an old blanket or a cuddly toy. You might have to organize quick washing of these comforting things so they are dry in time for bed.

Swaddling seems to have gone out of fashion. Many people relate it to bondage and imagine it is unkind to bind a baby's limbs so they can't move freely. A new interpretation regards this practice as restoring the restricted circumstances that the baby found comforting in the womb. Try it and you may be pleasantly surprised! You don't need special bindings; just tuck your child in the bed sheet a little.

A properly made bed is important. If the ends of the sheets or duvets are not tucked under the mattress, your child may move during sleep, become partially exposed and wake up cold or fall out of bed. Do you want to have disturbed nights because of this? No? Well you know what to do then!

Bodily contact is important at bedtime. With small babies try stroking their forehead from side to side with a couple of fingers while you cuddle your child to sleep. Pretend to be asleep yourself; lay beside them with your nose near their ear and let them hear your slow regular breathing. If your baby is struggling, hug their head and shoulders and leave their legs to kick at nothing. When all else fails, take them round the block in the car or buggy!

I don't recommend leaving children to cry themselves to sleep for long periods; no more than five minutes. Research indicates that this Victorian practice risks reducing their capacity to learn later in life. The stress of feeling abandoned causes the secretion of excessive amounts of the hormone Cortisol that can damage the developing brain. Child development expert, Penelope Leach, says, *"It is not an opinion, but a fact that it's potentially damaging to leave babies to cry. Now we know that, why risk it?"*

Dummies (comforters) are very useful for some children but others seem less interested in them. Apart from providing the child with a substitute for mummy's teat they stop up the hole the crying is coming out of! That's a win : win situation!

Very young children need naps in the daytime as well. Once again, bodily contact is important. I recommend learning how to put your baby in an African back sling, which leaves your hands free so you can carry on with your business; of course it helps if you have steatopygia – a big bum, like a shelf they can stand on!

GETTING UP

Mornings can become a trial. Although young children often wake up early they can be difficult to motivate into getting dressed and eating breakfast. It can be quite annoying when you have precious little time to get to work. You may not have the luxury of being able to ignore their obstructive behaviour and hope that it will go away, but I wouldn't respond by showing your annoyance – that's probably what they want! This is where you have to use your cunning and powers of negotiation.

Don't forget that questions will usually work better than instructions so, rather than, *"Go and wash your face"* try, *"Have you washed your face" "No?" "Are you going to, or do you want your friends to see it dirty?"* Get them to think of consequences.

If infants become distracted when you want to dress them try turning it into a game. Become a robot and walk stiff legged towards their wardrobe repeating, in a metallic voice, *"Clothes, clothes, clothes!"* "Jump into your pants!" works for a while – hold out the pants and let them pretend to jump into them.

Give these tactics a chance to work before moving on to other ones or you will spend your entire armoury in one go. If game playing is not working, try negotiating: *"When you are fully dressed you can have the television on until we leave for school."* Or, *"If you get dressed for me, I'll make some toast for you."* When you do this last one, you are letting them know that your contribution to their comfort and enjoyment has value!

MEALTIMES:

Who hasn't had a loud tummy rumble in an embarrassing situation? That's our body in action. We habituate our gastric glands to secrete their juices in time for lunch; if lunch is late they have no stomach contents to absorb them so they gurgle like bathwater going down a plughole. There's a risk the enzymes will do more than usual damage digesting the wall of the stomach itself. Doesn't that just indicate that we should feed at regular times of day?

Having smaller stomachs and higher energy expenditure due to growth and greater activity, tends to mean that children run out of fuel only a few hours after being fed; so it is important to get them to eat some breakfast, lunch and tea/supper. You will find that lunch is a more important meal for your children than it is for older adults who may be capable of lasting all day until evening dinner.

Children show different levels of interest in food. I've got one that isn't exactly ravenous. She is more inclined to play or suddenly need the toilet than to want to have her dinner. This hasn't stopped her growing so fast she has to wear clothes for six year olds despite only being four! Her younger sister, however, will make a beeline for any plate of food within reach!

Sitting at a dining table at least once a day is good therapy for a family. You all get a chance to learn how to behave at mealtimes including use of the knife and fork, to bond together in social chitchat about recent events in your lives, and, everyone will be inspired to eat fully by the example of the others. Talk about things you've done together – have some 'we' time!

Having scheduled meal times means not permitting eating between meals or your child will not be hungry. Try not to let them have high calorie snacks, especially not just before the food is ready. If your children really won't eat, you may have to try turning feeding into a game. Remember, constantly carping can destroy your child's natural wish to please, so try to make it fun. It's not just the old *'fork of food approaching the open mouth accompanied by train or plane noises'*; there are other techniques. Have you shown them how you can humorously attack food with growly biting? What about playing the blindfold tasting game? Don't forget, *"No ice cream until you've eaten your first course"* often works.

Sometimes they will eat things more readily if they had a hand in making them, so get them to help in the kitchen making faces out of vegetables on pizza or a *'potion'* (sauce) to pour over pasta. I have never found a child who won't eat jelly, which is good protein and you can put fresh fruit in it.

Diet can be a concern. When I was a child, postwar food rationing was still on in the UK. We had a good diet of freely available vegetables, unrefined bread, very little meat or dairy products and almost no sugar. My generation, now pensioners, still has mostly lean bodies as a result of not developing excessive numbers of fat cells when we were children. Once you have multiplied your fat cells they will scream out (hormonally) to be fed and expanded.

Fattening foods are plentiful these days, so we have to be more aware of the need for a balanced diet. When your child 'runs hungry' offer them some fruit or vegetable crudités as a snack rather than cakes or biscuits.

Try to avoid fizzy drinks – 'soda' is becoming recognized as a major cause of American obesity. Water, milk and real fruit juices are the best options but beware of liquids packaged to look like fruit juice that have a name including the word, 'drink'. 'Drink' legally releases a manufacturer from putting any more than a small percentage of actual fruit into the product; look at the small print and you may find you have been charged the price of fruit juice for a concoction of water, sugar, colourings, sweeteners and flavourings.

As part of the drive towards healthy eating, schools in England are now required to offer chips as a rare treat rather than the daily staple that they used to be. For parents, it's best to provide proper home cooked meals rather than fast food or ready meals which tend to contain too much salt, sugar, fat and other cheap 'food improvers'. Cooking from basic ingredients is much easier now you can buy ready chopped vegetables, salads and frozen ingredients; you can whip up a pasta or rice dish using a wok or microwave in about twenty minutes. Ok, you can fetch in a takeaway treat once a week!

Much nonsense is published in the popular press about different foods and drinks being 'good' for you one minute and 'bad' for you the next. Don't pay too much attention to their sensational articles – they are only trying to sell newspapers, just stick to everything in moderation and serve well-balanced meals.

Sugar is undoubtedly a tooth destroyer, contributes to obesity, may accelerate skin ageing and is implicated in the early onset of Type 2 diabetes, but there is no evidence to indicate that a little sugary food instantly turns children into wildly energetic maniacs! The body doesn't work like that!

Excess sugar that has been consumed is converted into glycogen and stored in the muscles and liver. The blood sugar level remains more or less constant; if it doesn't, you need to see a Doctor. Think about it – the quantity of fuel in your car's tank has no effect on the speed of the engine.

You just need to train your children to enjoy unsweetened food and then you can allow them to have, for example, a candyfloss at the fairground to avoid being called a killjoy! If you set the example by pulling a gruesome face as you reject a food that is too sweet and calling sugar-free foods yummy, they will probably ape you.

Flatulence can cause distress in babies and prevent them from sleeping. What we need to remember is that we are all subject to the force of gravity. A lot of wind consists of bubbles of swallowed air trapped in the bags and pipes of the digestive system; these bubbles will rise and escape through the mouth if it is uppermost. So don't try to feed your baby horizontally – hold them upright and they will not need 'burping'. If your child can't sleep for wind, get them to stand up and belch! Humans have evolved to be vertical!

Wind from the other end is due to gases produced during the fermentation-like process of digestion. They are the result of the action of trillions of bacteria, in addition to the human digestive equipment, and being upright will not help these to escape much, although standing on your head might! Belching and farting are good opportunities to teach social niceties. Although some societies regard a belch as a compliment to the cook, it may not get the same reception from polite company such as your local vicar! Many children develop their early understanding of comedy through these bodily functions.

KEYPOINT:

We all have a body clock – work with it not against it!

COMMUNICATION

We are now beginning to understand that several social animals possess the ability to communicate between individuals in their group. Many birds have such a good vocabulary of tweets they have developed local dialects! Imagine having a Glaswegian sparrow squawking in an accent that would be difficult to understand by one from Somerset!

Elephants have a rumbling debate between their leaders to organize group actions like drinking from a waterhole or saving a calf from drowning.

"These vocalizations facilitate the bonds between the elephants to be able to work together," said O'Connell-Rodwell of Stanford University School of Medicine, who has been studying African elephants in the wilds for 20 years. "It's the measure of an organized society. It demonstrates how another social animal grouping organizes itself through vocalizations."

http://m.phys.org/news/2012-10-elephants-hole-demands-conversation.html

Dolphins and whales also have a range of vocalizations that have different meanings and researchers are hopeful that, with the assistance of sophisticated computer programmes, they will soon be able to talk to them!

Humans have the best system of communication of all the animals. We can use gestures even before we have learned to speak. Your toddler will soon wave goodbye, come if you beckon him, sit down when you point to the ground - it's a bit like having a pet dog! Gestures however, change with fashion. I showed the flat of my hand to stop my toddler doing something and she obeyed on that occasion but, when her elder sister tried it the next day, she got high fived!

The start of talking is a great landmark for all parents – we gleefully report the latest utterances of our children. 'No' is often the first word to be said followed by 'mum' or 'dad'. Single words soon become sentences complete with intonation and accent recognizably originating from mum or dad. My eldest daughter's first sentence was *"What are you doing?"* The younger one is now attempting, *"I'm washing my legs"* and *"Can you get it?"*

Using a smart phone as a recording device is great for encouraging children to speak and learn new words. You will have great fun replaying these early attempts to them when they are older! When they start coming out with difficult words such as 'excellent' you have a great opportunity to praise. You might like to make a sound like a fanfare and call it 'Today's word'!

Try walking along the road pointing at parked cars saying, 'green car', 'red car' etc. Go to the window and say 'look at the bird' or 'see the rain?' Don't forget to get small - on a face to face level with your child. Of course this is when you have to clean up your own language!

With older children you can have a lot of language developing fun with a cheap pair of walkie-talkies.

KEYPOINT:

This is one of the best times you will have with your child - treasure these moments!

PART TWO: *EMPATHIC PARENTING*

A PARENT IS A CHILD'S FIRST TEACHER

A first child is always a bit of an experiment. Well, mum and dad may have had pets before but this one is a pet human! It's uncharted territory and, this new pet needs teaching!

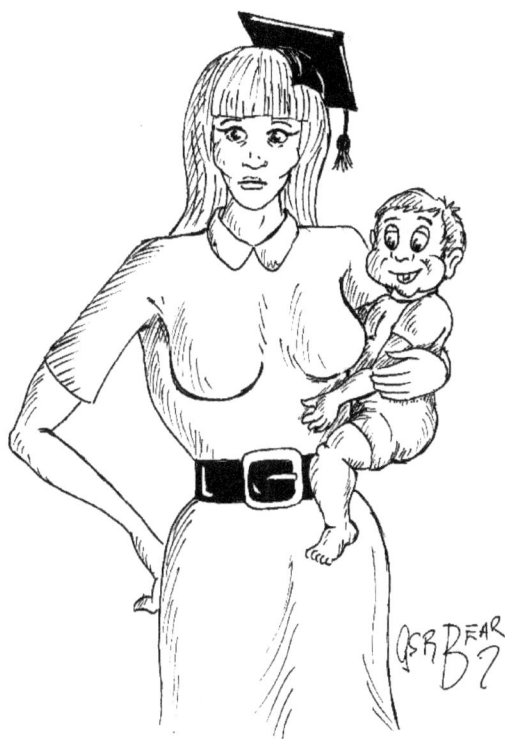

Modern Western society, being much more mobile than fifty years ago, means that the support of the senior members of a family, the ones with the experience of raising children, may not be close at hand. Most parents are under enough stress just being wage slaves to pay the mortgage or rent, then a baby comes along and they suddenly realize they have a whole raft of parenting skills to learn and they need to become amateur 'teachers' too!

There are two aspects to education – teaching and learning. Think of it as like broadcasting – there is transmission and there is reception. Transmission does not guarantee reception. For example, many radio stations are being broadcast right now and we are not listening to them.

Long ago, one of my colleagues unashamedly proclaimed in the staff room that he taught the same lesson to the top streams as to the bottom streams. Well, he may have delivered it the same but it must have been very differently received! Schools have been encouraged to recognize this in the last few decades and now have a teacher appointed to improve the delivery of lessons. No matter how appropriately they are taught, many children soon become past masters at ignoring adults or developing 'selective deafness' as many parents come to call it!

Children are at their most receptive in the early years. It's possible that the tone of their home life, up to the age of about four, sets their attitude towards human relationships. If they experience nothing but shrill arguments during that time, they may come to think that is the normal way for humans to interact.

From about four up to eight or nine years old they are easier to manage than in their teenage years. Early in my career, secondary school teachers used to loathe Year Nine (13 year olds) but that is coming down to Year Eight as children mature younger. We now know that the brain is being extensively 'rewired' at this period of life and that accounts for teenagers' reluctance to get up in the mornings too!

The period when they are in primary schooling is when they are more amenable. Yes, there will still be a range of abilities from those with learning difficulties to the outright academic, but communicating with them is only going to get harder as they get older. In the USA this is neatly expressed by a car bumper sticker that says:

'Employ a Teenager now while they still know everything'

The primary school age is when most children are more disposed to respect and admire adults and to wish to please them. When young, children are responsive to praise and pleased to be rewarded with smiley faces or stickers; you can even put a tally board on the wall and give them a coin for every five 'goods' they get. Later in life they come to think that most adults are fools!

This book concentrates on the primary school sector of childhood and the following sections are intended to help parents by explaining some parenting strategies and learning techniques that work best to produce a well-adjusted child.

KEYPOINT:

Parents can make a big contribution to their children's social development and education.

SETTING AN EXAMPLE

The tendency of children to copy influential examples puts parents under enormous pressure to set a good example; just think, you are being watched and heard while you do everything! It's like being on stage to an audience of your own child or children!

You will see your children toddling about with a pretend mobile phone at their ear before they can talk properly! Who do you think they copied that from?

When one of my frequent car passengers wanted the radio turned up, she used to say, peremptorily, *"Volume!"* Now she has become a mother she says, *"More volume, please."* She has realized that she doesn't want her children to copy her previously rude behaviour.

There was a BBC TV sitcom in the late Sixties called, 'Not in Front of the Children', the premise of which was loosely based on the notion that we should shield our children from many of the situations in the adult world. Having children does change our attitudes towards things like swearing and flirting, and may actually change our personalities as a result. We start thinking, *"I'm being watched; do I want my children to behave like this?"*

97

Recent research indicates that parental smoking is damaging to children's health even if the smoke is blown out of a window, and that's apart from the bad example it is giving. Alcohol consumption also has to be under control; we can't do our best parenting when drunk!

A heavy smoking, heavy cussing, hippy dad can turn into a paragon of respectability soon after the arrival of his child. He starts to realize that, although what he gets up to is more or less harmless in adult society, it would probably be better if he didn't swear and smoke in front of the children. It's surprising how a new parent's vocabulary soon changes from, *"You stupid son of a bee-itch!"* to *"Silly Billy!"*

98

Since our children are watching us, we have to become model citizens in everything we do. This type of consideration even extends to schooling. We may have very liberal attitudes ourselves but we probably want our children educated more conservatively. For this reason, most schools are not daringly liberal. Some experimental schooling systems with unusual levels of permissiveness were tried in the Sixties but they never became mainstream.

Head teachers know that what parents want is schools that are extremely conventional with smartly dressed staff and clear rules of acceptable behaviour. We even want teachers to be more dogmatic in the classroom than we would like them to be if they were guests at our dinner table!

The fact is, we have to prepare our children to fit into the norms of society ready for when they leave home. This includes dress code; as they get older, girls need to be made to understand the cultural significance of bare flesh and baby doll makeup.

I know a young man who couldn't get a job until it was pointed out to him that his unconventional hair-do might be off-putting to employers. I explained this limitation of freedom to him in terms of the assumptions that are made by others:

"Do you think you can change the attitudes of the rest of society? No? Well, you have a choice then, you either alter your appearance to fit in, or you take the consequences."

Of course we should be free to wear our hair in, for example, a cool dreadlocks style if we so wish, but we have to be prepared for small-minded members of society to judge us as a 'batty man' if that's what a Rasta appearance means in their home community.

Liberalisation can wait until children become undergraduates or leave home!

This mimicry may even extend to influence body shape – children of overweight parents are more likely to be overweight. Parents will put food on a child's plate using their own appetite as a guideline for quantity and children will copy their parents' eating and exercise habits.

KEYPOINT:

Children follow the example of their parents – you have been warned!

EXPECTATIONS

Expect your children to be good. Praise them when they are good. Have high expectations for their behaviour; don't expect them to be bad. This is so important it cannot be stressed enough.

Let's agree some targets of good behaviour. We would like our children to be kind, respectful to others (and to the personal space of others) and to be polite, wouldn't we? These are the lubricants that enable society to function smoothly. The opposites of those behaviours: rudeness, disrespect and unkindness lead to malicious relationships. The less malice, the better the society.

How are we going to foster the adoption of the good behaviours? Why not try reinforcing the empathy that our children were born with? Children start with a willingness to conform to the expectations of society; let's foster that...

Sir Keith Joseph, one of former UK Prime Minister, Margaret Thatcher's, policy gurus came up with a revolutionary new proposal for schools in the 1980s. Although I disagree with almost everything else that Sir Keith stood for, I have to give him credit for being the key mover in introducing a sea change in teaching style in the United Kingdom.

He suggested that we should stop criticizing and start praising! It sounds so obvious now doesn't it! The truth is, up until then the classroom culture had been quite negative, even antagonistic towards pupils; we aggressively belittled and berated them.

As a secondary schoolboy in the nineteen fifties and sixties, I had witnessed teachers throwing chalk at pupils or twisting their ears viciously, and I was aware of boys being caned. My teachers didn't do much teaching; mostly they *instructed*. Some of them were ex-military men.

Later, on my first day as a teacher, I was advised by one of my new senior colleagues to take a cane to my first lesson. He said, *"Pick on a boy whose tie is not straight and cane him there and then. You'll have no more trouble."* I didn't follow his advice and I did have trouble!

At another school the culture was for staff to pounce on any transgression, criticize every deficiency. Teachers covered students' written work with red pen crosses, wrote negative reports and generally got up the noses of the pupils and their parents! The strategy was to demoralize our charges into submission.

In private schools, indirect rule was established in those days by appointing powerful prefects. This was the technique that had worked for colonizing the British Empire! It was all about establishing, or in reality bluffing, that the United Kingdom of Great Britain was the powerful 'authority' and using local leaders as surrogates to save manpower! This was how 10,000 administrative officers had managed to govern the entire Indian subcontinent, which then had a population of 200 million.

Teacher's power was undoubtedly abused – one colleague wrote *"Oh Satanic Mills"* on a boy's report for no better reason than the boy's surname was Mills and this teacher felt pleased with the reference to a line in William Blake's epic poem, better known as the anthem 'Jerusalem'.

You're an imbecile Jones. What are you?

2+2=5

I'm an imbecile sir.

Some teachers even used what we would now term racial abuse! Back in the Seventies when the first black skinned boy arrived in our all white school, another teacher and I were putting our classes together to watch a Science film. In the blacked-out laboratory, my colleague quipped, *"Smile, Charlie, I want to see where you are!"*

It was an 'Us versus Them' culture in the classroom. Another of my colleagues planned lessons with the objective of *'taking up a bit of time'* – he saw the pupils as a problem that had to be contained not as children to be educated! In fact, the goal of many teachers was to occupy the children in some time-wasting activity to reduce the risk of acrimonious encounters. Many schools saw their primary task as one of producing subordinated, conforming, factory workers rather than creative individuals.

The last remnants of this Dickensian teaching style lasted beyond the Nineteen Seventies. Sarcasm and ridicule were considered legitimate weapons for teachers. Children were routinely criticized and their failures were pointed out to them. Reports to parents accentuated all the bad aspects of their children who became disheartened and discouraged by their schooling. Many people began to think that if they became successful after leaving school, it was *despite* their education not because of it. In interviews, parents said, *"I didn't do no good at school and it didn't do me no 'arm."*

The police had a similar attitude towards young people and took opportunities to scare them. One day, long ago, when I was about eleven, I cycled on the pavement past the Police Station. I heard a belligerent knocking on the inside of the station window and a policeman beckoned me to enter. Shaking, I went in to receive a dressing down for cycling on the pavement. Nowadays we advise children to cycle on the pavement because the roads are too dangerous!

Back then, parents threatened their sons and daughters with dire prospects of imprisonment and going to Hell. All of this was designed to belittle and subdue children and make them into the deferential society that was preferred at the time. Cinemas still played the National Anthem at the end of the movie to enable us to renew our subjection and loyalty to the Queen! This was the style of adult attitude towards children that was prevalent when Dr Spock wrote 'Baby and Child Care' in an attempt to bring about change.

Sir Keith Joseph's initiative came as a revelation. Suddenly we were invited to draw attention to what children *could* do not to what they *couldn't* do. We began to recognize that secondary school children came with skills and knowledge that we could develop. We started to encourage their

105

development with positive reinforcement: Praise. We began working *with* empathy.

The other side of the coin is the expectation of antisocial behaviour. If you, as a parent think you have identified, let's say, deviousness, in your child and you punish them for it, they may recognize that you are on the look out for deviousness and try to fulfill your expectations by supplying it. This is more likely if they feel they are not getting enough of your attention, in which case punishment becomes a reward.

Young children are not a threat but you can turn them into a threat by constantly correcting them. Then it might become a game; your child 'threatens' your tidy home in order to see you turn into a purple rage, you duly turn into a purple rage and your child feels rewarded.

Ultimately, parents like you and I would like to foster the development of civilized adults, wouldn't we? Psychologists consider there to be five crucial aspects of the wise reasoning that is characteristic of well-socialized people:

1. Willingness to seek opportunities to resolve conflict
2. Willingness to search for compromise
3. Recognition of the limits of personal knowledge

4. Awareness that more than one perspective on a problem can exist

5. Appreciation of the fact that things may get worse before they get better

If only more of our politicians and more of their electorate had those attributes! The raising of such paragons of virtue is obviously a long-term project!

I hope to help you, in some small way, to engage empathy in the task of raising your children. A big part of this is to have high expectations.

KEYPOINT:

High expectations should result in high quality results. Low expectations will definitely produce a lowly outcome.

LEARNING AND TEACHING

Learning happens in a learner's brain; they experience something and remember the valuable lessons it gave them. It happens best in the following ways:

1. OBSERVING AND COPYING (APING)

Like it or not, we are apes (genus: Hominidae). In 1860, just after the publication of Darwin's 'On The Origin of Species', there was an animated discussion about the kinship between apes and humans in Oxford between Creationist Bishop Samuel Wilberforce and Scientist Thomas Huxley. The dust has still not completely settled. Although the evidence supporting evolution is now indisputable, there are still pockets of Creationists who deny Darwin's Theory of Natural Selection and deny that we belong to the ape genus. Fortunately, reality prevailed in a 2004 court case in Pennsylvania, USA, when judgments were passed that forbids the teaching of 'Intelligent Design' (Creationism) as Science.

So, we are apes. What do apes do? They ape! What is aping? To 'ape' is to imitate the behaviour or manner of someone or something. That is how we learn a lot of things. We watch something being done and we copy it. I learned how to play the guitar by watching the lead guitarist in our local band. Even sparrows have learned how to eat peanuts from a bird feeder by aping the blue tits; they have watched and learned.

A couple of years ago, when I said, "I need to have a shave", my daughter, then aged two, used to say, *"I need to have a shave!"* Few of us realize the power we have over the young; humans are apes and we learn by aping. When they can't mimic an action identically, they *play* mimicry using an imaginary phone or steering wheel. Some dads may tell you how their infant daughter watched them in the toilet and then wanted to do a stand up wee! Such is the power of example to the very young!

Areas of our brains are equipped with 'mirror neurons' that, in functional Magnetic Resonance Imaging investigations, 'light up' in the same way when watching an action as when doing it. Parents can make this tendency work for them by demonstrating to their young children all sorts of stuff from how to wave a hand to how to hold a pencil.

People, particularly young people, just love to follow an influential example. This puts pressure on parents to set a *good* example. Social pressure is growing to require celebrities who become the idols of children, such as singers and footballers, to also set good examples. There is more on this in the Section on 'SETTING AN EXAMPLE'.

2. EXPLORATORY LEARNING (DISCOVERY)

Humans, like many creatures, are curious. We wish to investigate things. We love to open containers; you will see your toddlers opening your cupboards. We love to take things apart; just watch your one-year-old taking the coins out of your purse. We love to experiment; observe your infant child playing at mixing things like water and liquid soap. Children conduct a long series of what are, effectively, scientific investigations. Sadly, because this invariably makes a mess, adults drum this behaviour out of them! Maybe, in the interests of Science, the person looking after the children should not be the person clearing up after them!

"I'm talking about promoting science literacy and so the first step for the parents is to get out of the way. Allow the child to explore. If they start playing in the mud [and you say] 'Don't do that in the mud, I just cleaned those pants!' You're getting in the way of another experiment. If they start plucking the petals off the flowers you just bought from the florist and you say 'Stop that! I just paid $10 for the flowers" Had you let that continue they'd find, in the middle, the stamen and the pistil and they'd learn something about the flower. For 10 bucks that's cheap!" **Neil de Grasse Tyson**

There is an old adage attributed to Confucius: "I hear and I forget, I see and I remember, I do and I *understand*." Such wisdom from two and a half millennia ago! Human nature hasn't changed much; we still learn much more from doing than from listening or seeing. Watching a video of how to do up a nut and bolt is no substitute for using a spanner yourself and feeling the resistance of the thread. How else will you find out that it's usually better to begin rotating anti-clockwise until the starts of the threads 'find' each other? How else will you learn to avoid cross threading and doing damage? Once learned, you will apply this knowledge even to doing up coffee jar lids!

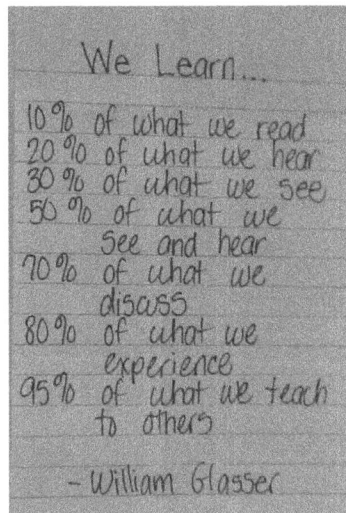

We Learn...

10% of what we read
20% of what we hear
30% of what we see
50% of what we see and hear
70% of what we discuss
80% of what we experience
95% of what we teach to others

– William Glasser

What do *you* do when you get a new gadget? Do you carefully read the instruction manual or do you get it out of the box and plug it in? I think I know your answer; we prefer learning from making our own mistakes to reading instructions or listening to someone telling us how it should be done. That's why manufacturers cleverly make their gadgets intuitive – children can use a touch-screen phone from about one and a half years old.

It's no wonder then, that discovery is a good learning technique. The difficulty is getting the teacher or parent to resist the impulse to show the child how to do something and to stand back and simply watch as they find out. Early in my career as a Science teacher we mostly did demonstration

113

experiments then, later on, class practicals became the fashion; we just set a problem, gave out some equipment and watched the children get on with it, while monitoring for safety.

More recently, I was one of three adults watching our small children building sandcastles. The other two grown-ups kept offering a barrage of advice while I just watched the children build and saw them find out about how the wetness of the sand had to be just right, how you had to tap on the upside down bucket to get the sand out and so on.

Leaving them to discover and keeping your hands off what the children are doing takes will power! It tries your patience since you have to watch them struggling to do something that you could do much quicker yourself, but to keep intervening makes you sound like a nagging know-all. You do not want that reputation; it will simply accelerate the development of your child's tendency to ignore you!

Allowing discovery to happen can mean leaving them to find out the hard way but the lessons learned really will be better remembered. One cold day, my eldest daughter insisted that she didn't want to wear a cardigan and a thick coat. Her raincoat would be enough, she claimed. Ok, I let her have her own way but I told her that, if she wanted to ignore my advice, she wouldn't be in a position to complain about being cold. As we walked to the bus stop, she started to say, *"I'm c..."*, I looked pointedly at her and she realized what she was doing and changed it to, *"I'm wondering when the bus is coming!"* I got a warm scarf and gloves out of my bag for her to put on. She had learned for herself and I had avoided an argument with a four year old!

WHY ARE THESE LEARNING TECHNIQUES EFFECTIVE?
There are three probable reasons:

1. The learners are learning by choice – these horses have led themselves to the water! That means they are willing learners - motivated and engaged.
2. Nobody is pontificating at them patronizingly; modern learners don't like feeling belittled by a superior.
3. They enable the opportunity for the learners to make their own mistakes and learn from them; these are always the best lessons.

Willful creatures aren't we!

TEACHING TECHNIQUES
Teaching is an attempt to expose children to experiences from which they might learn. Teaching in schools is difficult because it often has to go against the flow; information often

115

has to be delivered under the opposite of the preferred learning conditions. Lessons may have to take place in the absence of the ideal circumstances under which Good Learning occurs; that is, without allowing learners the freedom to investigate and make mistakes for themselves.

Sometimes teachers will have to face towards the class and pontificate; that is not a natural situation except for an entertainer and teachers often have to deliver material that is the opposite of entertaining, like algebra!

Teachers are not given just one or two children from a family to work with; they are given a class of about twenty or thirty unrelated youngsters of roughly the same age. A few members of the class might be interested, a majority might be indifferent and some might be resentful. The resentful ones may mess about and try to spoil the experience for the rest of the class. When that happens, the educational content of the lesson may have to be sacrificed in the effort to control discipline.

Fortunately, most children understand that teaching a class is a special situation and they make allowances! Thanks to this there are some teaching techniques that can be reasonably successful! The best teaching techniques allow a child to feel (or fool a child into feeling) that they are cleverly responsible for their own learning. These are described in the following pages.

1. GUIDED APPRENTICESHIP

This is a strategy derived from the Observation and Copying learning technique (aping). If a person who is good at something has ever shown you how to do it, you have been a beneficiary of Guided Apprenticeship. Being shown how to play 'Chopsticks' on the black notes of a keyboard is probably the most common example. If you made cakes with a parent, you were getting Guided Apprenticeship.

The relationship between the Guide and the Apprentice is paramount. It's a technique that works well as long as the expert doesn't patronize and belittle the apprentice. Once the relationship becomes unequal, your children may get to the stage where resistance builds up, they may then decide that they already know enough and will start to argue with you about how it should be done. Years ago I was asked a question by a fourteen-year-old boy whom I was tutoring at a Special Needs Unit; he said, *"Why do they make us keep coming to school at my age when we know everything?"* He was serious!

If you want to be sure not to offend a bigheaded child's pride you can get them to watch while you guide someone else such as their younger brother or sister, or maybe you can ask another adult to act the part of the apprentice. That turns it from a teaching experience into a purely learning experience of the observing and copying kind. The watcher can choose to identify himself with the expert not the learner.

I call this 'Proxy Learning' and it allows children to feel good about achieving *for themselves*.

Television production companies have latched on to this technique; the first cooking programmes to be broadcast consisted of a presenter cooking to camera, some more recent ones show a presenter showing a member of the audience or a celebrity how to do it.

Obviously, Guided Apprenticeship is more easily delivered in a one to one situation than to a whole group of kids. However, a teacher can teach a few children and then get them to teach the rest while watching to see that it doesn't go the way of Chinese Whispers! Chinese Whispers is the name for how messages get mutilated as they pass through several messengers. The classic example tells about the General who received a message from the frontline. He was told, 'Send three (shillings) and four pence, we're going to a dance!' The message had started out as, 'Send reinforcements, we're going to advance!'

The ripple outwards strategy relies on Peer Tuition:

"Self-education is, I firmly believe, the only kind of education there is." **Isaac Asimov**

2. PEER TUITION
After an expert, the next best person to show you how to do something is a novice like yourself! It's not quite the blind leading the blind because, in this case, your colleague has

just discovered, or been shown, how to do whatever it is themselves. This means they have a fresh understanding of the problems of learning the task.

What makes peer tuition so good is that it is an equal relationship, in other words there is virtually no gulf of seniority, knowledge or ability between the tutor and the pupil. Michael Baum, Professor Emeritus of Surgery and visiting Professor of Medical Humanities, University College London, calls this phenomenon of asymmetrical relationships the "gradient of power". Most of us don't like to feel subordinated; it affects our self-esteem and confidence. Unless we have an iron clad ego, we don't take kindly to being told stuff by someone superior. We will accept being tutored by a peer much more readily because we know he is not in a position to ridicule us and make us feel small. Peers are less open to being accused of patronizing.

Peer Tutors may be novices at the task they are tutoring and may have no particular teaching skills but they do have something very powerful. They have just learned to do it themselves so *how* they learned is fresh in their minds – they know where you can go wrong and how to help you get it right. And they are your mate – you will be a team!

The Peer Tutor is actually benefitting too – there is no better way of reinforcing a new skill or new knowledge than by teaching it. Recent research shows that the tutor actually gets more from the experience than the tutee. We should encourage children to tutor each other more often. At home, parents can get an older child to show younger siblings and, sometimes, vice versa if the older one is prepared to play along. When a younger child is reluctant to wash, get their older sibling to set an example – they will probably copy!

Peer Tuition is not to be mistaken for Peer Pressure, which is an, often detrimental, pressure to conform to the Herd Mentality that mostly affects teenagers.

2. MULTISENSORY TEACHING:

Confucius's saying, ("I hear and I forget. I see and I remember. I do and I understand.") presaged the modern teaching technique known as Multisensory Teaching.

This technique suggests that, if we can feed information to the brain through several sensory routes at the same time, it is more likely to be learned.

"Engage the five senses!"

The idea is to engage sight, hearing and, if possible, touch, taste and smell simultaneously to assault the brain with the same information. The expert thinking suggests that this strategy will obtain maximum attention, maximum interaction and therefore, maximum understanding and remembering.

If you've ever tried to have a conversation with a child who is gaming on a Playstation or Xbox you will know how wrapped up they can become when they are watching, listening and responding manually to the game simulation. This is known as Deep Immersion. More needs to be done to make use of this level of concentrated involvement in education.

The Multisensory Teaching technique is applied in the early stages of literacy teaching when a child is exposed to the sound, the sight and the feel of letters. Input in the form of nerve impulses go to the brain from the eyes when they see the letter, from the ears when they hear the letter sound, and from the muscles controlling the fingers when they trace the letter shapes in sand (Proprioception, the limb position sense is largely unrecognized by the public). Tablet computer apps are good for this.

Unfortunately, it is quite difficult to involve many senses to teach some things. Often the nearest we can get is to use the multisensory power of song and dance. See the Section 'MOOD, MUSIC AND DANCE'.

ONE TECHNIQUE THAT DOESN'T WORK SO WELL:
OLD STYLE TEACHING:
When I started Science teaching in 1967, I did the same as I had seen my school teachers do for me. That is, I stood at the front of the laboratory and talked at the class while making chalk marks on a blackboard. I didn't know any better and, after all, it had worked for me in the Grammar School and right up to graduation.

Back then society, budding rock stars apart, was *deferential*. We had grown up in post war austerity Britain when parents, teachers, policemen and adults in general were respected. There were no televisions, X Boxes, iPads or Smartphones so school was the best show in town! Men in military uniforms were commonly seen, many of our teachers were ex-servicemen and school atlases still had a third of the world coloured pink to designate the British Empire.

When the liberal attitudes of the sixties eventually spread to the provinces, we all stopped fearing establishment figures and started questioning and disrespecting authority. The result is that modern children, and adults for that matter, don't like being *told*. Instruction only works in the armed forces.

We now know that the lecturing style of delivery is only suitable for about 10% of the population who have a natural disposition to learn in that way. The other 90% are uncomfortable with it. There is more on this in the Section, "WHY DON'T YOU DO AS YOU'RE TOLD?"

THE FUTURE:

What is needed is a revolution based upon 'mastery learning'. For schools, I see great promise in the concept of "flipped classrooms" being piloted in California where the focus is on learning. In this model, pupils study their lessons in their own time, from videos, podcasts and eBooks, which will become the primary methods of content delivery and, the following day, they work on assignments in class with the assistance of a teacher in a computer room where the teacher's monitor gives access to every student's screen. Lessons become 'homework' and 'homework' is done in class! Each child can learn at his or her own speed until they master a concept. Teachers can mentor students and enlist the help of advanced students as tutors. Team building skills are developed.

DON'T BUY:

Don't buy unsupported theories. There have been several that became popular: Gardner's 'Multiple Intelligences' concept, for example.

In 1983, Howard Gardner suggested that there are several different aspects to intelligence. He believes in eight 'cognitive abilities': Spatial, Linguistic, Logical-mathematical, Bodily-kinesthetic, Musical, Interpersonal, Intrapersonal and Naturalistic. He also considers that Existential and Moral Intelligence may be worthy of inclusion. Well, if he can't be sure whether to include Existential and Moral abilities in his list, why should we pay any attention to his other eight items? They are obviously just his choices! I'm sure you can tell from my use of words like 'suggested', 'believes' and 'may' that we are dealing with mere opinion here.

In fact, recent evidence indicates that the major component of intelligence is due to a single core ability. Clever people probably just have better processors in their heads and they will most likely be better at everything. You can find many examples of such polymaths; my favourite is Queen's virtuoso guitarist, Brian May, who abandoned a PhD in Astrophysics when Queen took off in 1973 and came back to complete it in 2007! Yes, It's now Dr Brian May!

When I was Chairman of the Governors of a primary school, we had an Educationalist come and talk to us. He explained that, in his view, children came to school with a blank brain and, given a good education, everyone had the potential to achieve everything. When he finished speaking he invited us to write down questions, which he said he would answer after we had coffee. I wrote, *"Since all sexually reproducing species exhibit variability in every characteristic, what evidence do you have to suggest that all babies are born with the same intellectual capability?"* Sadly, although he answered other questions, he never addressed mine! That was when he lost my respect.

Then there is the 'Index of Learning Styles' developed by Richard Felder and Linda Silverman in the late 1980s. According to this model (which Felder revised in 2002) there are four 'dimensions of learning styles'. They propose that some of us learn better from pictures and others from words, some like a linear sequence of information while others prefer to see the whole thing at once, and so on. It's another model unsupported by convincing evidence; the clue is: Felder revised it!

Ok, I accept that there are natural abilities; there are gifted musicians and artists, but in the early stages of trying to raise a child you haven't discovered yet what talents he or she may have. Therefore, instead of worrying about which 'learning style' to target, you'd be better off continually varying your teaching techniques to maintain interest.

Even famous child rearing guru, Dr Benjamin Spock, did a deathbed retraction of his doctrine of allowing children to express themselves unfettered by discipline. He said:

"We have reared a generation of brats. Parents aren't firm enough with their children for fear of losing their love or incurring their resentment. This is a cruel deprivation that we professionals have imposed on mothers and fathers. Of course, we did it with the best of intentions. We didn't realize until it was too late how our know-it-all attitude was undermining the self assurance of parents."

Beware of gurus! (I'm a practitioner, not a guru, of course!)
I confess I go along with Dr Spock to the extent of not using

physical punishment (there are better forms of punishment, see section on 'Sanctions') but my strategy differs in that it accentuates the enhancing of empathy, responsibility and *self*-discipline, and includes a lot of parental cuddling!

As your child's parent and first teacher, why not use some of the tried and tested teaching and learning techniques at home?

KEYPOINT:

Teaching cannot succeed if it involves heavy compulsion. Pick your moment, be sensitive to how the relationship is proceeding and stop when either of you is tired. **Always remember, good teachers show you where to look but don't tell you what to see.**

"What we learn with pleasure we never forget."
Alfred Mercier

PARENTING STRATEGIES

If you want to see parenting strategies that *don't* work, watch the Chipmunk movies! The whole premise of their storylines is based on the Chipmunks naughtiness and how their hapless manager, Dave Seville, fails to cope. See the following example:

Alvin: *"When are you going to stop treating me like a child?"*

Possible Responses:

A) *"When you start behaving like a grown up."*
(This was the *answer* actually given in the film 'Chipwrecked')

B) *"Right now."*
(This was the *strategy* actually tried in the film)

C) *"I've never treated you like a child."*

Which is best?

Response C! Because then the question doesn't even need to be asked!

SOME GOOD PARENTING STRATEGIES.

I recommend trying to foster the development of responsibility and self-discipline by tapping into the natural empathy that we are all born with. There follows some things parents can do to promote this aim:

1.   *Give Them Your Attention.*

Your children badly want your attention. Spend time, have fun together. Time is your currency. Build up credit. In an ideal world you should always have time for your children. Remember, you can't teach children anything, even how to behave, unless they *want* to learn. If they don't feel they are getting the goods, which in their minds is your attention, there will be nothing to withdraw as a punishment.

> *"Listen earnestly to anything your children want to tell you, no matter what. If you don't listen eagerly to the little stuff when they are little, they won't tell you the big stuff when they are big. Because, to them, all of it has always been big stuff."*
>
> Catherine M Wallace

How do you give someone attention? Please don't think I am patronizing you – some people genuinely don't know. Watch how salesmen and teachers relate to people – it's about showing interest, it's about eye contact, it's about listening to what they are saying without interrupting and responding appropriately, it's about having an open body posture –

folded arms says 'I'm not interested in you or what you want.' You won't sell anything that way, not even your attractiveness as a fun parent.

When your tot toddles towards you with his arms held out, pick him up! If your child asks for a cuddle, stop what you are doing and cuddle them! You need to *look* at your child, engage his eyes! Use your animal magnetism! Don't be looking at your emails and leaving your offspring to speak to the back of your head. Claiming to be listening to what he or she is saying while you are not looking at him or her is not the same; they will see from your posture that you are not interested however much you may deny it.

If your infant son says, *"Watch me kick this ball"*, please do so. He is asking for something we all desire: a show of interest, which might be interpreted as affection. Even President George W Bush wanted the Pressmen to watch him tee-off on the golf course! Show some reaction to your child's attempts to engage your interest; show pleasure; learn to act it, if necessary!

"Sincerity - if you can fake that, you've got it made."
George Burns

131

It's more than rude not to pay attention, it's demoralizing; it's damaging to your child's self-esteem. Your child may start to feel unwanted and uncared for.

Two things may happen to children who feel unwanted. Firstly, they may imagine they have to try harder to get your attention, which means they might think they have to do more risky, naughty or outrageous acts. Secondly, they may cease to respond to punishment; if they perceive themselves to be not worth caring for, why should they care what happens to them? The next thing you know, they are self-harming.

"When you got nothin', you got nothin' to lose"

Bob Dylan

'Like a Rolling Stone', 1965

So, please don't be always on your smart phone or using your tablet computer – that removes you from the home society. It's an insult. Your body language is saying, "*I don't really want to be with you, I have this other world which I can get enjoyment from – I laugh at something on my screen, you don't even know what I'm laughing about, and I don't care!*" These devices are such recent additions to our lives that we are still working out the appropriate etiquette.

Once you are in the habit of giving your children your

attention you can move on to giving them joy! It just means doing something like catching their eye across the room and putting your tongue out to make them smile! Have a secret communication with them! If you've built up a reputation with your child of good times spent together, your attention can even be promised as a reward; to get them to do something, such as getting dressed in the morning, try this tactic: *"Do this for me now and I'll play football with you later."* How inexpensive is that?

One way you can have fun together is by 'rough and tumble' - play fighting. Throw your small child on the bed! Grab his foot and pretend to eat it! Ask if he's got any ketchup! Lie on your back, put your toddler face up on your belly and raise your legs saying, *"Legs up!"* They will copy you even before they have learned to speak. *"Legs down!"* *"Right leg up!"* *"Left leg up!"* It helps them learn language.

Watch how mammals play with their cubs for inspiration. You can use play fighting as an opportunity to introduce the concept of 'Pax' (Peace) for when one of you wants to stop. Tell them, if either of you has had enough, all you have to do is say, *"Pax!"* or show crossed fingers and play will stop. Incidentally, Pax originated back in Roman times with the sign for the supposedly peaceful new Christian religion – the cross of the Crucifixion; this was before the Crusades!

Another good way to develop an enjoyable relationship is to engage in imaginative play. Tell them if they fall off the bed they could get eaten by the crocodiles but you will rescue them and pull them back from the jaws.

Some children naturally do fantasy play, often adopting the role of a mother or father, sister or brother. See if you can get a part in their drama and act the role to the hilt. Make suggestions about props you could use or scenes that could help the story develop e.g. sit on the sofa and say, *"Let's pretend we're going to school in the car now"* and make engine noises. It is possible to be both parent and playmate, they will understand that you are role-playing like them; there is no need to act like a self-important Victorian martinet.

Fantasy play can be used as a parenting tool – if your daughter starts playing mum to her dollies, you can say, *"Come on 'mum' eat your dinner and set a good example to your kids!"*

Sometimes, children's demands for your attention can become intrusive; they might, for example, sing loudly when you are trying to have a conversation with another adult, or kick up a racket when you are watching the News. If you tell them to stop it, they will know they've succeeded in getting your attention - they've won! To see how to manage this type of behaviour, look at points 3 and 4.

2. *Reward Them When They Do Something Right*

Be sure to reward good behaviour whenever possible, show your children they can shine! Find any tiny opportunity to praise them and compliment them for doing something good. Invent chances to do this if necessary: *"You've put your shoes on the right feet! Well done!"* Don't do this after they have learned about sarcasm though!

Rewards can take the form of a smile, a kind word or, if they've been really good, you can draw a smiley face on their hand or on the reward board you have fixed to the wall, give them a stamp from an inked rubber stamper or award them a sticker or certificate. Save confectionery for really special occasions – you don't want them to develop a sweet tooth and there are so many alternatives that your child will find acceptable; it's always a good idea to have fruit available. See more about this in the section on Sanctions.

The other piece of advice I have to offer in connection with children doing something right is, 'If it's working, go lurking!' By that I mean, if the activity your child is engaged in is harmless and they are finding it enjoyable, leave well alone.

Try not to interrupt or demand that they stop. As much as possible let sleeping dogs (and active children) lie!

3. Ignore Them When They Are Naughty

Sometimes, if your children see you are watching while they do something naughty, or if you respond to their activity with correcting language, you are giving them what they want! They may have been deliberately fishing for your disapproval! By expressing it, you have rewarded them; they have got your attention, you may as well have given them a box of chocolates! Seeing you watching them may even have spurred them on to greater efforts of naughtiness!

I know this is counterintuitive, but it is often better to express your disapproval of inappropriate behaviour by *withdrawing* your attention. You can do this in a passive way by not looking at them and not answering them. This takes a lot of patience and works best if it's just you and one child; if other people are in the room, your child may not even notice you are blanking them! Then, you may have to *tell* them you are not going to do stuff with them if they behave like that.

The next stage is to throw your child a LOOK. If they are in the habit of looking for your approval or disapproval, catch their eye with an expression that makes it clear which they can have.

"Throw them a look!"

Or you can escalate to active ignoring: move yourself out of the room (if they are old enough to be left alone or if there is another person present) or ostentatiously do something else – tablet computers are useful when you want to appear engrossed (as long as that is not your normal activity). Obviously, you need to monitor a situation for risk: you don't want to be using the ignoring tactic while they play on the edge of a cliff!

If you have another person in the room with you, try behaving conspiratorially with them; whisper in their ear! Talk about your child inaudibly but raise your voice slightly to reveal his or her name. Let out the occasional louder word like *'ice cream'* or *'Disneyland'*. You will be surprised at how quiet your child suddenly becomes in their desire to eavesdrop your conversation! This also works in a noisy classroom. You can even have a pretend conversation on your mobile phone and achieve the same result! Thank heavens for nosiness!

Whisper, DISNEYLAND, whisper.

Ignoring them can be our most powerful weapon. If you habitually have fun together, your children will miss interacting with you. OK, it's not always effective but it's often the best tool we've got!

4. Fighting Fire with Fire

The opposite tactic can also be used. When your children kick up a racket during your favourite television programme, try turning up the volume! Point out that, when they are watching their programme, you do not drown it out with noise and spoil it for them. Tell them that, if they want the volume turned down, they need to be quieter so you can hear it. If they get in front of the screen, do it back to them when they are enjoying watching something. Getting them to understand another person's point of view is enhancing the empathy they were born with.

You can extend this strategy to unwanted physical contact. If they start pinching you, tell them that, by their action, they have now permitted pinching and pinch them back (not hard!). If you have an enjoyable physical relationship with them, involving tickling perhaps, this will not come across as malicious or threatening. Tell them that, if they do something to someone, the message they are giving is that aggressive action is permissible in their world and therefore it is only fair for that person to do it back to them. This might make them think before they attack! Fairness means the same number and type of contacts, of course.

With a really tough child it might be beneficial to show him just what damage you are capable of doing by impressively crushing a beer can whilst emitting a lion-like roar(!) or punching a cardboard box so that they can see how you are using restraint in your dealings with them and, just maybe, they might start using restraint themselves. Have you tried tearing an apple in half? That's impressive!

It's OK to use tickling as a tactic to get them to stop doing something. My eldest daughter was covering my mouth when I was trying to speak to a friend so I tickled her to get her to move her hand away. In between bouts of laughing, she said, *"Stop it!"* I replied, *"It's you who needs to stop it, I'm just retaliating."*

5. Be Consistent

Don't send mixed messages – don't sit at the dinner table showing off your ability to toss peanuts up in the air and catch them in your mouth one day and then tell your children, *"Don't throw food!"* when they try to do it themselves the next day.

If you have rules with associated punishments or rewards, be consistent. Always have the same punishment and never miss delivering it. *Known consequences* can help with developing self-discipline. If they can remember being deprived of fun for a particular transgression before, as in, *"Last time I made us late in the morning, I didn't get taken swimming after school",* they may think twice before doing that again.

Stick to your rules yourself. If you have, sensibly, made it a rule that you will not drive off until everyone is seat belted and, you've said that if anyone undoes their seat belt when you are moving, you will stop at the first opportunity until they do it up again, don't be the person who breaks the rule! You will not help yourself if you show disregard for your own rules.

6. Manipulation

The word 'manipulation' has had a bad press. It actually should be applied to techniques used to help grease the wheels of society. Young Chimpanzees attempt to manipulate each other, human children are born with a propensity to enjoy trickery – manipulation has evolved and it has been a driving force in the development of intelligence. We all do it and are exposed to the attempts others to do it to us. Advertisers, politicians and priests are notable practitioners. Look at the intention behind it to determine whether it is malicious or beneficial.

What sort of a relationship with your child do you want? Do you want to be continually correcting them and telling them what to do and what not to do? Are you trying to set up an unequal relationship of Master and Slave? Or are you prepared to trick them into doing what you want without disagreement? If so, just make it *fun!*

Although, as you will see a little later, I don't recommend allowing children to divide and rule their parents, I regard it as perfectly all right to use that tactic against *them*! (British hypocrisy?) Surely there's nothing wrong with using comparisons like this: *"Your sister has eaten all her dinner, why can't you?" "Our guest is being good, isn't she?"* (Hint, hint!) *"I'm going to play with xxxx, he's good at sharing."*

Once you find out what they like doing you can use that to your advantage. When they don't want to do what you ask, try to turn it into a game. For example, my eldest daughter said she wanted me to go upstairs with her to get her socks. I didn't want to go but I knew she likes running so I said, *"I'll chase you!"* then I moved rapidly forward a couple of steps clapping my hands together to raise the excitement level and she ran off, coming back a few minutes later with her socks.

When you have two children you can use one to manipulate the other. Here's how – our two year old daughter was being difficult to get into her buggy so I asked her five year old sister to get in it knowing that she is possessive about her things. Sure enough, the young one said, "My buggy!" and

142

pushed her sister out of the way to get in it. Mission accomplished with ease!

Counting is another way of turning things into a game that they might do more willingly than they would simply obeying your request; *"I bet you can't get your socks before I count to ten!"* All you have to do is count loudly to three as they run off and restart counting from eight when you hear them returning!

Once they discover the fun of doing things at speed you can use the stopwatch on your phone and challenge them to set a time. Would daddy like his slippers brought downstairs from the bedroom? Ready, Steady, Go! Mummy needs her slippers too – see if you can beat your record! Well done, stand on this podium (footstool) while I put a medal round your neck and hum the national anthem!

Young children do not have a long-term plan for their activities – they flit from one thing to another. Well, parents can do that too! If your child is doing something you want them to stop, try flitting! In a supermarket, when your child is being a pain, try the counting game as a form of distraction – *"I bet I can get to the apples in twelve giant paces!"* They will probably want to join in counting and pacing because it sounds like fun. Whatever annoyance they were up to is forgotten.

Distraction is a great way of getting them to stop doing something. When your toddler grabs hold of your phone, wallet, purse or whatever, don't get involved in a struggle to get it back off them. Offer them something else as an alternative. It doesn't have to be a bribe. Hold out a ball, the chances are they'll take the ball and release the phone. Fair exchange is no robbery!

When your infant is being a nuisance somewhere public and you have no toys to distract them with, use your car keys! To a child, a bunch of keys is a fascinating toy. Just be sure to get something else to trade in time for when you want them back or use the 'tickle release'!

If you don't have a ball or anything to trade, try something like, *"What's this amazing bird out of the window!"* or *"Who is that character on the television?"* If there are other people around, get them to play along; everyone could go over to the window and look out. In their curiosity, they might drop the keys or allow you to take them back unnoticed. Magicians use this technique (misdirection) to get you to watch the wrong hand when they 'disappear' something.

It's always better to phrase these diversion attempts as

questions. That way you are avoiding the natural tendency to disobey an instruction and invoking your child's natural curiosity to get them to do your bidding. Questions are much better than instructions in lots of situations. *"What's that over there?"*

Another way is to use what, in theatrical circles, would be called a 'prop'; try blowing up a balloon and releasing it or doing a quick conjuring trick! Click your fingers like a castanet! Buy a book on card tricks and learn some! Learning how to disappear a coin and recover it from behind their ear is a wicked tactic! While their attention is elsewhere, you can get your phone or keys back!

Alternatively, pretend to go along with them and suggest they should put the phone somewhere for safe keeping so they can find it later, and then, surreptitiously remove it! They may forget about it and never notice that it's missing. If they do discover it's gone, you can say with a smile, *"There you are, things can go missing, that's why you need to keep them safe!"*

There is so much in the world that is new to young children they can be deflected from what they are doing very easily. When my eldest daughter complained that her young sister had captured her favourite doll, I said, *"Just give her something else!"* She did, and got her doll back.

Once you get used to turning your child's resistant behaviour into a game with *your* intended outcome you soon become an expert at it. To get a reluctant child to walk to school you can make it a race to the next tree or lamppost and call out, *"I'm winning!"* You can 'hide' behind the lamppost with bits of you sticking out both sides so you look silly. Try pretending you don't know each other and are meeting for the first time!

Once your child starts to have opinions, you can try to manipulate their choices! My youngest daughter doesn't like bananas but, naturally, she wants to have whatever her sister has. So, we give them both half a banana, the older one eats hers and the younger one just holds it. I asked the big sister to take her little sister's banana away. I said, "She will say, 'Mine!' and start to eat it." When this little play-let was enacted that is exactly what happened. We laughed as she ate her hated banana! Why did I ask her elder sister to try to take away her banana and not do it myself? Because of the imbalance of power: she may have just handed it over to a large adult but was bound to contest her sibling's attempt at possession.

A teacher friend of mine tells how he was at the hairdresser's when a young mum came in with a reluctant toddler. The little boy didn't want to have his haircut; he wriggled dangerously when the scissors came near. My friend produced his distraction techniques. He put his spectacles up on his forehead then, pressing his nose like a button, twitched his forehead to make them fall down onto his nose! He borrowed a dustpan and 'hid' behind it popping out to say, ' Boo!' Eventually the hairdresser gave the boy a comb and he calmly investigated it until she completed the job.

His 'Boo' technique was a variation on the old game of 'Baby gone'. This is great fun with toddlers – they love to have their head covered with a sheet or towel while you say, *"Where's baby gone?"* and immediately reveal her/him saying, *"There (s)he is!"* There will be much laughter!

You can use, *"I bet you can't"* as a technique. For example, *"I bet you can't hop for ten hops in a row," "I bet you can't walk like a robot,"* and things like that. Join in with the challenge yourself if you can.

When they start scooting and cycling you have more possibilities. The route to pre-school for my daughters involves a short piece of road with no pavement so I challenge them to keep safely between the double yellow no parking lines.

When they begin to learn the alphabet you can play I-spy but, before then it can be 'first one to see' as in first one to see a red car, first one to see a blackbird, first one to see a cow or our home, etc.

If you have time, it's a good idea to learn some children's entertainer tricks; things like making funny noises with your hands or mouth, making an envelope into a monster (picture on page 134) and using misdirection in the style of a conjuror. OK, all of this is Tricking but, you cannot shield your children from deception for very long and it's far better they should meet it from a loving parent first.

As they get older and start creating their own agenda, your techniques will have to adapt to get them to do your bidding. This is when you need to negotiate. For example, if one of your children wants to feed the ducks and the other doesn't, offer a deal, *"If you help us feed the ducks we'll take you to the play park with the zip-wire afterwards."*

The alternative, forcing your child to do your bidding, will only generate resentment and your relationship will be the worse for it.

7. Engaging Empathy

Try to make your child aware of others feelings, how others

perceive him or her and how they might react to what your child says and does. Put them into others' shoes. Get them to think about the messages they are giving out.

"Are you going to eat all the biscuits on you own?"
"Is that mean?"

"Why are you scowling?
"What does that look like to your friends?"
"See your face in this mirror (or smart phone)"
(The old tactic of saying, *"If the wind changes, you will stay like that!"* is useful in this situation and it even has some truth in it – as we age, our faces develop creases from frequently used expressions.)

When the older one doesn't want to watch the baby TV channel, remind them that you, an adult, watched it with them when they were little and now it's their turn to be kind to babies!

Repetition is the key to acquiring the skill of being considerate. The more often a child is encouraged to think about their actions before they commit them, the more likely they will automatically default to the mind set of considering the options *before* doing or saying something hastily that they may regret later.

Any activity that requires a child to think about the alternatives before making the next move reinforces the value of listening and watching for new information. If they have lost the ability to listen, to really pay attention, playing a game such as draughts or chess will help them to regain a sense of how important the latest, most up to date input can be to good decision-making.

Anytime a child is engaged in an activity where they must take in current information and imagine what their opponent might do next in order to make a considered decision, they are learning to think critically and empathically. Teach them to think before they act!

Grandparents can be useful here! Getting your children to understand that elderly people need to be treated differently when they have mobility problems or pain requires an extra level of consideration.

8. Set the Ground Rules Beforehand

If you can predict that parenting difficulties might be coming up in the future, try to pre-empt them by setting the rules in advance. For example, as you drive to the theme park say, *"When we get to the gift shop you can have one thing only."* Timing is of the essence here, if you can get your message to your child when they are feeling positive about being taken out, they will accept conditions much more readily. It's the same psychology that politicians use when they put out bad news during good times!

Without ground rules, shopping can become a nightmare at the checkout. If they pick up something you don't want to buy, wait till you get to the checkout – they may have forgotten about it by then, and you can sneakily leave it behind and hope they don't miss it until too late! Keep to your own rules too, you can always come back later and buy more when they are not with you!

When your child picks up something in a shop I know the temptation is to be on tenterhooks to tell them to put it down immediately and to argue against their disobedience, but try to chill out a bit - give them the chance to put it back themselves. If you walk away they may replace it and follow you. Walking away is often better than going after them, which can become a game of chase! Don't be over reactive. Try not to make obedience into an issue – they are your children not your slaves!

You will have to explain to them that when they pick up something from the supermarket shelves it's not theirs until it's been paid for at the checkout. Let them give it to the checkout person themselves and see it being scanned and the payment happening. Soon you will be able to give them some money to spend themselves.

If you want to move on, don't keep repeating, *"Come on"* say, *"Goodbye"* loudly and set off - they will most likely follow you!

9.   Humouring them

When they are very young, many children want to help. My advice is: try not to refuse their help. It may be inconvenient, they may make a mess, you may be able to do the job much faster without their 'assistance' but a time will come when they won't offer. That's likely to be when you *do* want their help, so take it while it's available!

Find your children something to do when you are baking, for example. Get them in a little apron with washed hands and ask them to stir the cake mixture or cut out the gingerbread men from the biscuit pastry. It's good training for responsibility and they will feel important. The traditional reward for helping is to lick the bowl out!

If your daughter wants to play waitress at dinnertime, go along with her. There may be a few spills to clear up but she has to learn about serving food on to her own plate, so to do it at home is a good opportunity. You can usually find something safe and easy for them to help with. Mushrooms can be safely cut with a blunt knife, for example. If you are slaving over a hot wok, maybe they could carefully lay the table. We got a mini broom for the girls to join in with sweeping when they see an adult doing it.

Remember, our children wish to ape our behaviour and they wish to do things with us, so to refuse is more than churlish, it's a parental rejection. Parental rejection is a punishment technique and shouldn't be associated with an offer of help, which is not naughty behaviour, but an act of kindness. If you do have to refuse an offer of help, give a reason such as, *"This is dangerously hot or sharp or I'm using strong cleaning fluids."*

On the subject of parental rejection, what do you think is the worst possible parental rejection? Answer: divorce. Well, *separation;* children are not concerned about the legalities. Just think, the message you are giving your children is that your life would be better without them in it. Nobody has to point this out to them – they will get to an age when they can work it out for themselves. It's worse than bereavement since the dead cannot continue to reject by choosing to live somewhere else and deny their presence daily.

10. Mockery

On one occasion, when my infant daughter threw a tantrum, I tried ridiculing her by mocking her behaviour. I lay on the ground crying and kicking the floor! This was so unacceptable to her that she smacked my arm! That was obviously how she thought that sort of behaviour ought to be dealt with!

"Throw a tantrum!"

Don't let them use crying as a means of getting their own way. If your child turns on the crocodile tears don't give in to their demands, try ridiculing them! When I do an exaggerated wail back at my daughter she reacts so disapprovingly I sometimes get a slap. Hopefully she gets the message that I disapprove of her doing it just as much as she disapproves of me doing it.

Another tactic, which sometimes works, is to appeal to your child's sense of humour: *"Get out of my child's body at once, you nasty alien!"*

BUT IT'S MUCH EASIER TO DO THINGS WRONG!
Here are some of the ways parenting can go wrong:

1. *Impatience: the enemy of good parenting!*
Children know all about delaying tactics! They will slow right down and hope that you will give up trying to get them to do whatever it is. They will try to 'wind you up' or use distraction techniques on you! They will do anything to try to get you off the job of insisting that they do your bidding.

Just see them go into slow motion when it comes to going to school or at bedtime! Suddenly they will become interested in reading a book, watching the TV, tidying up, anything to avoid doing your wishes. They will discover a fascination for something they previously didn't like, even being nice to their younger brother, if they think it's preferable to what you want them to do! Treat it as comical; if you get annoyed, they will have won.

Try to stay cool and play along with them. For instance, say something like you'll join in reading with them if they get into bed now. Go and lay on the bed with them to get them started. You have to be prepared to put into second place your own desire to watch post-watershed TV and drink wine, in order to invest time in raising your children. There is more on this in the section: 'Daily Routine'.

2. *Falling for the divide and rule tactic employed by children.*

We've all seen children playing off mum against dad. From a very early age they learn to ask one parent for permission first, then, if they get denied, they go and ask the other in the hope of getting a more favourable response. Fend off such attempts by saying, *"I'll discuss it with your mother/father and see what he/she says."*

It's always difficult having two leaders - one usually has the upper hand. It's an elementary mistake that can even be made by politicians - the two Davids (Liberal Leader, David Steel, and Social Democrat Leader, David Owen) found it impossible to present a united face for their Alliance in the 1983 UK General Election. In the home this can lead to the *'wait till your father/mother comes home'* scenario.

Schoolteachers get together in a meeting and corporately decide policies of attitude towards difficult pupils. The home would benefit from doing the same. It's best if all the carers are interchangeable. Stick together; don't disagree. Try to have the same approach to all situations. It is very important to *support each other*.

If you want to have an argument with your partner, don't do it in front of the children; wait until they are in bed, then do it *quietly*. If necessary, debate your disagreement by texting; you might find that method keeps tempers more in check as a bonus!

3. *Failing to accept help.*

You have to be prepared to let go of the reins and accept help from other adults who have your children's best interests at heart. Allow other people to correct your children, to identify mean behaviour as mean, for example. Remember, according to the African proverb, it takes a village to raise a child and the village needs to appear united in the task of instilling appropriate conduct.

Never take your child aside and tell them not to listen to their babysitter, teacher, uncle, aunt or grandparent. What message does that give a child? You might as well spit on the other adult - the child will know who is boss and who is worthless. You will be seen as the big gun. Don't expect your child to ever behave well for a person that you have so badly undermined.

It's rather like your uncle opening his front door to find an irate neighbour demanding that he stops entertaining his nephew so loudly. Your uncle wants to tell the neighbour to get stuffed, but he's brought a policeman with him! How will uncle feel? Emasculated? If you want to be an authority like that policeman, you may find it hard to get uncle to babysit ever again!

Particularly, do not tell off an adult for reprimanding your child *in the child's presence*. That just turns the other adult into your puppet. She or he will have no power in the eyes of the children who will play up like crazy until the real authority, *you,* returns.

No one will teach for long in a school where the head teacher does not support his staff and parents need to support other, carefully selected, carers too.

In the days of the 'open campus' policy in the UK (before the 1996 Dunblane school massacre), schools occasionally had situations in which a parent or elder brother would turn up behind their child to confront, or even threaten, a teacher. Once, a man barged into my class and threatened me, waving his fists, because I had sent his naughty younger brother to stand outside the door of my laboratory and the boy had strayed off into the playing field, which was then open to all and sundry. The Police were called and they identified him as a known local troublemaker and drunk. Nowadays you can't get into a school without an appointment.

If you have a bone of contention with another adult, take them aside and explain your point of view *privately*. If you support other adults, like grandparents and teachers, together you will raise a nicer person.

4. Intervening too little

Unfortunately, in recent decades, too much attention was paid to Dr Spock's permissive parenting guidance. It's easy to see why the good Doctor came up with the advice that he did; his book was written in reaction to the nineteen thirties parenting tradition of *'spare the rod and spoil the child'* (Proverbs 13: 23 - 25). He lived in a climate of severe parenting which did need to change.

There was a strange contradiction in his book because, although he discouraged strict discipline (which a lot of parents wrongly interpreted as meaning their children should have no discipline), he also advised no affection! He said parents should not pick their children up, kiss them, or hug them, because that would not prepare them to be strong and independent individuals in a harsh world.

159

So, no discipline and no cuddles – no responses at all! The result was a generation of children who felt ignored and couldn't get attention from their parents no matter how hard they tried to act up! No wonder the Sixties era of free love and drugs came along! The deprived teenagers were casting about for the experiences and affection that they had been denied as children.

I know it's a hackneyed expression but you can 'kill with kindness'. If you create the impression in your children's mind that they are never wrong they will repay you with obnoxious behaviour. Don't think you must only say nice things to your child to protect their supposedly fragile egos – that's what turns them into obnoxious little brats!

Please reprimand your precious child - we all need guidance when we are growing up, and do feel free to criticize your children - it's part of the free speech rule in the society they will grow up to live in! If they are being unpleasant company, and they will be sometimes, let them know! If *you* don't, you can be sure that, in another situation, someone else will!

However, there are ways of doing it. Do it by questioning if you can, *"How would you like that done to you?"* Try to avoid the boring instruction, *"Don't do that!"* It will most likely be ignored anyway. See Section: 'Why Don't You Do As You're Told?

5. *Being too authoritative*

Dog owners reading this will know that dog training has recently moved away from the old technique of establishing dominance over our pets, such as was promoted by BBCtv dog trainer Barbara Woodhouse in the 1980s, to a reward based strategy. We have now realized that centuries of breeding have actually changed the way man's best friend thinks; domesticated dogs no longer behave like the pack wolves they came from. We don't have to show them that we are 'top dog' because they are now born with love for people; they want to do tricks for us just for praise and the occasional biscuit. They respond to the tone of our voices and some of them are misogynists – they behave better for the deeper sound of a man!

Our own offspring are much the same when they are young. Up until puberty, they want to behave acceptably for their parents and adults in general; we have been selected by nature to learn to discipline *ourselves* to be nice to each other, within our own communities at least.

Authority takes this away. An authority says you don't need to discipline yourself because it will discipline you; if you transgress you will be punished. Under an authority, discipline is imposed *externally* - the responsibility for your behaviour belongs to the authority, not to you. Doesn't that sort of license you to test out the boundaries?

There are four problems with this:

FIRSTLY, an authority responds *after* the event - it can't *prevent* transgressions, unlike self discipline, unless it instills an undesirable level of fear by the use of terrible punishments such as execution or the cutting off of hands! Also, the culprit has to be identified, caught, charged, tried and found guilty before any punishment can be enforced, by that time any connection between the crime and the punishment has become tenuous.

SECONDLY, it perpetuates juvenility - an authority subordinates its subjects and delays their maturation.

What follows is rather counter intuitive but, hopefully, will make sense as you read it!

If you treat people like naughty teenagers, they will behave like naughty teenagers (at least until their metabolism slows down in middle age). They will attempt something naughty and wait to see if they get caught. It's exciting. It's fun!

Think what this means: *Authority INVITES Transgression!*

Encounters with authority can become an expected part of the naughty child's daily routine, a desired form of interaction or entertainment. It can even become scheduled to specific times and locations - coming home late, for example.

Soon the naughty children may start seeking the authority figure out and baiting him just to enjoy an acrimonious encounter. Confession time: as small boys, my mates and I used to trespass on an old man's allotment just for the thrill of having him chase us.

Later in life I saw many novice teachers create trouble for themselves by trying to impose an unenforceable level of discipline. Their classes became a hilarious riot of uncontrollable pupils ganging up to taunt the hapless staff member.

If a transgressor doesn't get caught and punished, they will (wrongly) assume they have the approval of the authority to repeat a particular naughtiness. They typically say, *"You didn't say I mustn't do it"*. (Respond with, *"You didn't ask if you could!"* – shift the blame!) They will become repeat offenders and increase the risk of getting caught. The more the authority has repressed them, the more excitement will be available for daring to transgress!

In the case of young children who are exposed to a forceful authority, the children's lives may become dominated by a 'Rule Culture', which they may start to emulate by making rules of their own. Suddenly they may announce that nobody is allowed to play with their toys or enter their room. Aping a parental example is what children are programmed to do, so, in a house where a parent imposes lots of rules, why shouldn't they make up some of their own? Inevitably, family life suffers.

If your friends start telling you that you are too strict on your children you may respond by saying how you have to be like that because they are so naughty. Please stop and ask yourself, *"Is it me who has made them like that?"* Children love to react against authority so try not to provide them with the authority they need to react against!

Extending childishness in this way makes more work for the authority; it has to stay in control for more years of a youngster's lifetime. What are you going to do when they grow up and reject your punishment? If it is to continue to be effective, punishment has to escalate in severity as time goes by and as children grow up, just ask dictators. The longer you impose control over their lives, the longer will be the period of estrangement between when they reject you and when they come to forgive you.

THIRDLY, it introduces a requirement for reasonableness and fairness because an authority risks losing respect if it is seen to be unfair and unreasonable. This loss *will inevitably happen* because perfection is impossible to achieve - the fairness will always be open to accusations of favouritism and the reason will sometimes have to be, *"Because I said so"*, if only because that is the best level of understanding achievable within the time available.

In the adult world, since it accepts responsibility, an authority must also accept blame and when, in the perception of the aggrieved, it fails to deliver the expected high standard of justice, calls for a revolution soon begin to be heard. This sort of motive drove much of the 'Arab Spring' of 2011; an authority is on a hiding to nothing.

Self-discipline, on the other hand, invites no comparison with how others are treated; it abides by its own internal standards.

FOURTHLY (and this has already been alluded to), a time will come when the authority loses the willing submission of its subjects. In the case of children they grow up and need to crawl out from under the protective umbrella of their parents.

To retain its superior position in the absence of willing

submission, an authority has to respond with the enforcement of more severe punishment. More severe punishment may give the transgressor a reason to have a grievance, and, if the authority is the State, a feeling of victimization – *"Everyone is against me."*

Then we have a real problem - a person who considers himself to be 'uncared for' will have a 'don't care' attitude. He thinks he has evidence that he is worthless. He now has a license to behave extremely antisocially - he is beyond the law because he doesn't care what punishment might happen to him.

In fact, he *desires* punishment – it's the only attention he can get. When he does get punished it merely confirms his impression that all of society hates him and that he is alone. This vicious circle of positive feedback means that, for those who reject it, authority actually *causes* malice and *justifies* it in the minds of the perpetrators of misdemeanors. Punished pupils will say, *"I'm not doing any work for that teacher!"*

The stricter the discipline, the more severe the revolt will be when it does happen; in extreme cases it may become a cause for which people will be prepared to die. Together with injustice (also often the result of overbearing authority - see above), this can be the origin of, and motivation for, terrorism. If a state authority escalates its response with more force it invites the description 'tyrannical' and starts attracting international disapproval. These developments do not make the world a better place.

Western societies (it's different in China) have moved away from the attitude of deference to the militaristic style of authority that was prevalent in the middle of the war-torn twentieth century. So, although authority and punishment are necessary to deal with the odd psychopath, for the above reasons, they should both be kept to an absolute minimum or they will become part of the problem.

In some sense, every time you discipline your child, you are giving a twist to an elastic band; eventually the tension may become unbearable and it may snap. My advice is don't intervene unless really necessary. Ask yourself, *"Is what they are doing dangerous or causing any harm?"* No? Then why not permit it? Oh, it's making a mess? That's a great opportunity to introduce 'Tidy Up Time! Put some music on and work with them to clear up. It could be their favourite hit recording. Tidying could actually become fun! They could earn a sticker!

A wise parent or teacher will teach their children self-discipline, not inflict an authoritarian regime on them.

5. Treating them like children

Don't talk about yourself in the third person: *"You've upset Grandpa now!"* If you talk down to them, the implicit message you are giving them is, *"You're a child, so we expect you to be naughty and we make allowances for you to misbehave."* You are almost giving them permission to be bad!

You are inviting the response, *"I can't do that, I'm a child!"* to your request, *"Help your sister do up her seat belt, please"*. Don't let them use their age as an excuse for rudeness or bad behaviour! Don't give them that weapon to get out of family chores.

Treat them like little adults. Expect them to fit in as good members of society by engaging their empathy. Encourage them to put themselves into other people's heads. If they ask *"Why do you put ice and lemon in your water?"* respond with, *"Why do you think?"* Get their interaction; treat them as equals.

Everybody prefers to be consulted rather than told; it makes them think their opinion is valuable and they feel important. People with high self-esteem are much less likely to be antisocial; they have no resentment because they have no grievance.

168

To guide them in the development of self-discipline, ask, *"How would you like that done to you?"* Point out to them that, if they punch or kick, they are telling everyone that punching and kicking is acceptable in their world so it must be all right for people to do it to them, including their parents (although of course you won't do it hard!).

I'm not suggesting that you should be entirely stand-offish on your adult pedestal. It's perfectly ok to play childishly with your child when the moment is right. My daughter asks me to *"play mums and dads with our hands"* and I'm happy to do so. My left hand becomes 'mum' and I speak with a high voice as I open and shut my fingers and thumb as her 'mouth' while my right hand is 'dad' with a deeper voice. We enact a little playlet about getting our kids ready for school or going on holiday. You can use sock puppets for more realism then, if you have no socks nearby, you can have a laugh about mum and dad being naked! Your child will recognize that play is not reality.

There is one area where you should recognize their childishness. That is in the matter of their size and ability. Obviously you should get down to their level and help them when they are struggling to dress or feed themselves. It's sometimes necessary to talk into their ear when trying to get their attention. I've even resorted to, *"Earth calling daughter!"*

When your children get a hero, a performer who becomes a role model, ask, *"What would he/she do?"* If we get them in the habit of considering others, maybe they will become considerate. What do you think?

6.   *Try not to be correcting all the time.*

Here's an example: our toddler filled a bag with fruit from the fruit bowl and wandered into the sitting room with it. Nanny stormed after her, angry with the improper movement of fruit. I said, just let her do it, in her mind she's shopped at the greengrocer's and is on her way home. What's the worst that can happen: a piece of bruised fruit?

Ask yourself, what sort of a relationship do you want with your children? Try not to be always complaining and correcting. It is easy for a concerned adult to be looking for non-existent dangers to warn their children about. Too much correcting either leads to a life of continual conflicts, or, like the boy who cried wolf, the message becomes blunted and ignored.

For example, if your children won't eat their meal, as long as they are not anorexic, don't nag at them, simply point out to them that they may be hungry later and food won't be available then. Later, when they say, *"I'm hungry."* Say to them, *"Well, you've CHOSEN to be hungry – you didn't eat*

170

your meal." In this way we might get our children to think of the consequences of their actions.

Try not to hastily jump to conclusions. If a child does something annoying, don't respond immediately; that may be what they are after! Ignore it for a while and give them a chance to get bored and stop of their own account. You may be surprised how soon this happens with some children.

One common childish response to your expressions of concern is, *"I don't care!"* My advice is to respond to that with, *"Sorry, we only want caring people on this planet!"*

Modern children (and adults for that matter) don't like being continually *told and controlled*, but they have been naturally selected, over hundreds of thousands, if not millions, of years of evolution (depending on where you want to start counting), to be empathic, which leads to reasonably good behaviour. If you have no other strategies than continually correcting, you will soon find yourself in an acrimonious relationship with your children. Hope that, with your guidance and example, your children might pick up self-discipline.

Remember, you are actually moulding the final touches of your child's personality! The attitudes of the next generation are in your hands! They will remember the parenting style you gave them and use it on their own children later in life. This is the nearest you may get to social engineering!

Some of us may be born with smaller egos than others. Continuously correcting those children won't help. You should attempt to enable your children to approach the norm - not massively big headed and not excessively introverted. Encourage your children if they are too timid and point out the risks if they are being too bold.

KEYPOINT:

Too many points to summarise here! You need to internalize most of the above to be prepared for the inevitable eventualities!

RIGHTS AND RESPONSIBILITIES

There is a slippery slope between rights and responsibilities! Toddlers often start wanting to do things for themselves – let them! Let them feed themselves, dress themselves and toilet themselves – they want to learn how to do these things. Some children will become quite annoyed if you continue to try to do things *for them* like you did when they were babies. You will have to be patient while standing back because these things will take much longer for them to do than when you did them and they will make more mess! While they wish to become responsible, it's very important to encourage it; the time will come soon enough when they *don't* wish to accept responsibility!

Help them to become self-catering while they are willing; when they want a drink, show them how to get one for themselves. If you don't do this when the opportunity arises, you risk turning yourself into their servant. The ability to demand service becomes a right in their minds, 'Get me a drink!' – you will turn them into little princes and princesses. It is possible to 'institutionalise' your own child in your own home and find yourself becoming a carer pushing a large idle child around in a buggy as if (s)he is an invalid!

When they become teenagers you can expect them to avoid or deny responsibility at every opportunity – *'It's not my fault!'*

173

'You do it!' 'I can't do my homework now!' 'I'm tired!' 'I don't feel well!' etc. That's why you need to encourage responsibility while they are young; you never know, the habit you instill now may stick later or, some of it might…

Some of the European Welfare States have fallen into this trap. These nations set up their benefit services for 'free' (i.e. state provided) health care, education, pensions, unemployment, etc in the aftermath of the Second World War when there was an acknowledged need for the state to be generous to its returning heroes. Two generations later some members of the public have assumed that they no longer need to be responsible for their own welfare at all! Why should they when they know that the state will look after them? They have their *rights*, don't they!

It now appears that the system ought to have been set up with a small contribution being required at the point of use in order to give the users a feeling of ownership of it. Unfortunately, that would not be a vote winning policy today! Hindsight is a wonderful thing!

KEYPOINT

Cash in while you can!

ARBITRATION

As a naive young man, I went into teaching because I wanted to be a teacher; it was only after I started work that I discovered I had to be a care-worker, policeman, judge and prison warder too!

You will discover that one of your jobs, as a parent, is to settle disputes between children. Your child may come up to you saying, *"He's chasing me!"* Your response should be, *"Well, stand still then!"* Nobody can chase someone who is not moving!

"She called me names!" is another frequent complaint. Tell them to ignore it. After all, it was just a fleeting vibration in the air. There are no bruises! Obvious racial, sexual or class-based insults should be seriously disapproved of though.

Many people, not only children, don't realize that being offended is a choice. Offence is more taken than given. When you choose to take offence you are effectively giving your antagonist a weapon that, until then, he wasn't sure he had! If you choose to take offence you are weaponising him! If he then deploys the weapon you have given him, you can blame yourself (although you will have identified someone who has malicious intent towards you). Now that he knows you are offend-able he will repeat the offence for his own amusement! If you choose not to be offended you will disarm him; it's your choice. Taking offence is like shooting yourself in the foot – it's a boomerang grenade!

At the Special Needs School, where I taught for a couple of years, name-calling was a major pastime. The most common way for the pupils to insult each other was by impuning their mothers, *"Your mother's a whore!"* This happened so frequently it became contracted into *"Your mother!"* The rest was implied; everyone understood!

There will be lots of occasions when grievances will be brought to you for solving. With children under three years old, you can get away by using the distraction technique. Just change the subject – do a flit, and all will soon be forgotten. This won't work when they get older and you will be expected to act as investigator, judge, jury and executioner!

It's usually best to take a complaint seriously unless you can tell that the complainant is trying it on; you will get to know the regular complainers! Go through the motions – it may seem like a trivial event to you but it is probably very important to them!

Always try to get both sides of the story – interview all the participants and any observers. Point out any discrepancies in their accounts and try to resolve them by further questioning. Seek agreement and apology.

Ask the culprit how he would feel if he had been treated the same way and try to get them to make up. If they won't agree to play nicely together, you may have to separate them into different rooms or assign them to the supervision of different adults for a time to cool off. If you are on your own, you may have to change the situation in which the disagreement occurred, *"Well, if you can't play nicely, I'm taking the ball away and we're all going to sit down and watch a DVD quietly."*

KEYPOINT:

This is part of parenting; get used to it!

TRANSPORT

Traveling with kids is fraught with problems; they start when you are getting ready to go. Here's a tip, pace things sensibly and set the example yourself. I've watched mothers shouting at their children to get dressed when they are watching TV an hour before departure. What's the reason for that? It's false urgency. This just reveals that the mother expects to be able to bully the child into doing her will just because he or she is a *child!* Children have no respect in some households.

How you handle this critical process can determine the tone of the day and, if it turns into a regular acrimonious event every school day morning, of your whole relationship. My technique is to give a slow countdown as departure time approaches and be visibly preparing myself. Chances are when they see me putting my coat on they will realize the urgency themselves, unless the concept of urgency has been turned into 'the boy who cried wolf' by repeated false urgencies. So what if they miss the start of the film once? That's a good way of learning the lesson of meeting a deadline.

Do you recognize the following?
Child, *"Are we nearly there yet?"*

Parent, *"Well, 'nearly' is a relative term; compared to Antarctica, we are indeed very near!"*

Child, *"How much further is it?"*
Parent, *"All the rest of the way!"*

Child, *You're lost aren't you!"*
Parent, *"Not at all, I know precisely where we are. We're right here!"*

Child, *"I need a wee!"*

If you can't remember having conversations like these with your parents, your own children will soon remind you!

Always, always, always get them to go to the toilet before you leave! Do this religiously or suffer the consequences! Motorway service stations can be miles of no-stopping road apart and there is little you can do in an unfamiliar urban area other than find a place to park near a public toilet; what's the chances of that? In the countryside, boys can be sent to pee behind a roadside tree but girls doing the same will get wet feet and legs! I made my daughters a 'Shewee' by cutting the bottom corner off a bathfoam bottle to overcome this problem! With small girls you can also perfect the technique of holding them in a seated position in my arms and pointing their posterior to direct their jet safely away! Girl as water pistol! (NB point them downhill!)

Regular two hourly stops at roadside services are necessary whether requested or not. You will find the functional importance of these facilities changes from being filling stations to being emptying stations! You may be able to extend the time interval by insisting on no drinks in the car – "If you're thirsty, have a grape/orange/apple."

"Emptying station!"

On long flights it's also important to take your small child to the toilet regularly irrespective of whether they want to go. Infants frequently misjudge the urgency of their bladder's messages and you don't want to be waiting in a queue with urine trickling down your child's legs!

Recently, I traveled from Auckland, New Zealand to Heathrow, UK with my four-year-old daughter. Anticipating toilet problems, I had packed five pairs of pants and three pairs of leggings in our carry-on luggage. By the time we got to Sydney airport, just the first, shortest flight of the journey, she had wet three of the pants and all of the leggings! When we arrived at Dubai airport they were all used up and she had to continue without underwear! Luckily, I had put her in a long dress but I was in trepidation of her doing a headstand in a Muslim country!

With two or more children, when they get big enough to sit beside each other in a car they will surely fight! Put siblings in a confined space and this is inevitable. You can try insisting on the concept of personal space but, probably, you will need to separate them into front and back seats. That may be why the people carrier was designed with three rows of seats!

Try to have lots of ways of entertaining your children on boring journeys. At five plus you can play word and number games – try making words out of the number plates of the traffic. If you can afford it, get them a handheld electronic games console each.

One problem that I predict you will experience is forgetting to take things. You will have set off and a child will wail, *"Where's my dummy?"* Or you will get to the car park with a sleepy child; open the boot, and NO BUGGY! What to do? Buy another one? Go back to get it? Piggyback your child to the nearest supermarket and put him in a trolley?

As the trip comes to an end you need to be aware of your children's level of exhaustion – you want them to have enough energy to walk to where you've parked the car. How will you stop an activity before they will need carrying? Promise an ice cream!

Got stuck with no buggy and a toddler who is getting fractious in a shopping mall? Is she tired of walking but when you pick her up she goes rigid to stop you carrying her in a seated posture? My advice is to use the shoulder carry. If you sit them on your shoulders the height is a bit exciting and scary for them so they stop struggling and let you hold both feet and both hands so they feel safer. Give them a dummy and you might find them falling asleep on your head as you walk along! The worst that can happen is they might dribble in your hair!

If they don't fall asleep you can try getting them to walk again but if they retract their undercarriage as you lower them to the ground that's a clue that they don't want to be put down!

Things can be forgotten on the return journey too. A favourite dolly gets left in the hotel, a sleeping bag at a friend's house, one shoe drops off as you wheel your child around town. I have no remedy for any of this! Nobody I've ever met has been perfect enough to prevent it happening!

Maybe we should take a leaf out of the Boy Scout's book: 'Be Prepared'!

KEYPOINT:

Traveling with children can be a trial – you may find that you like to stay home much more than you used to!

SOUND, MUSIC, DANCE AND MOOD

I saw many young teachers go into a classroom and start teaching in a shouting voice. When they got cross they had nowhere to go – their voice was on maximum already. The next week they were off work with a sore throat. At one school two senior teachers were retired early with permanently damaged larynxes.

Good teachers have normal, or even unusually quiet voices so the children have to be quiet to hear them. Parents would be well advised to adopt a low volume level as their normal voice but to be prepared to project louder when immediate attention is required, such as when danger presents itself.

We are all affected by sound, children particularly so. Observe your children in a room with a television on; they might have no interest in the programme until some music starts, then their attention will probably be grabbed. Advertisers know this and often include a hit pop song in their commercials.

It's not just a catchy tune that can set a mood but the tempo as well. 'House' music is good for young people to dance to because it has about 120 beats per minute. The tension of the revealing of the results in a talent show is often enhanced

185

with the rhythm of a heartbeat (lub-dup) – about 70 pulses a minute. Slower rhythms, such as in lullabies, are good for damping down excitement and soothing children to sleep.

Music aimed at the young tends to be faster, about 110bpm; just listen to BBC Radio 1 and compare the tempo to Radio 2. Since I'm a 'fogey' now, I like music to be my 'brain balm'; I can do without excitement!

Singing is very useful as a bonding activity. Sing with your children – you do not need to have a great voice! You can do this anywhere: walking to school, in the car, at home, and at any time of day. It will help your infant child develop their speech and memory.

Dr. Daniel Levitin, Professor of Psychology and Behavioural Neuroscience at McGill University in Montreal, Canada, says the combination of rhythm, rhyme, and melody provides reinforcing cues that make songs easier to remember than words alone. Another academic, Dr Williamson, a memory expert at Goldsmith's College in London says, *"Because music can be encoded in so many ways, it's what we call a 'multi-sensory stimulus'"*. This is why we recite nursery rhymes to help toddlers learn to speak.

When I was a much younger man, I was in a four-piece band:

keyboards, guitar, bass and drums with three part harmony vocals. We played round the hotels and clubs near the West Sussex coast and it was magic fun! Practicing enough to be able to simultaneously play an instrument and sing is a totally involving experience. The more difficult something is, the more rewarding it is to achieve it. We got good enough to be able to step back from the microphones and talk to each other while still playing.

That gave me a legacy; I can now appreciate music on many levels, following one instrumental part or another rather than just the vocals, but it makes it hard for me to enjoy rap. Why would you throw away melody and harmony to leave behind only chanting to drums? Primitive tribes could do that; surely we can do better in the twenty first century! Ok, I'm a fogey!

Thanks to playing (badly) the guitar, bass and keyboards, I have more than usual control over my fingers. This means I can touch type speedily, using all my digits, which makes writing this book a pleasure! It's all in the brain; we all have the same fingers, we just need to learn to use them individually by practicing. Please get your children involved in musical instruments as young as possible and they too will benefit.

Dance is also multisensory – that's why it is so enjoyable; our brains love to have plenty of input. If you want to torture someone, remove all stimuli. This is called sensory deprivation and it can make people go mad. My mother had an elderly friend who first went blind and then deaf. The poor lady continued to live for some time in a care home. What a nightmare.

Girls seem to like dancing more than boys. I have a hypothesis about this; it is a survival mechanism! Many creatures perform a courtship ritual, which is a precursor to copulation and human animals are unlikely to be an exception. Maybe our girls are merely learning how to flaunt their bodies enticingly from an early age! Recent research indicates that lap dancers move more sexily and earn more tips when they are ovulating! Get your daughter enrolled in dance classes to channel this interest to good use.

Activity is good for us. People who do not accept a challenge but just sit around watching television are not called 'couch potatoes' for nothing; research shows they are statistically more likely not only to become obese, with all the attendant health risks that endows, but also to develop early onset Alzheimer's disease.

Work is also good for us; it gives us a purpose and a feeling of self worth. The long-term unemployed are in danger of becoming institutionalized in their own homes. The brain is similar to a muscle in that one respect: you use it or you lose it.

Music and dance both affect mood. Mood is infectious, particularly to children. Children feed off energy. Many years ago I knew an extrovert young teacher who was like a pantomime performer in the classroom. He wound his pupils up and then he calmed them down before winding them up again! When he was off sick, nobody could follow his act!

To influence your children you need to 'set the tone' for the desired behaviour. Placid parents will get their children to settle more easily, fidgety people will transmit their nervous energy.

When your children get too excited, challenge them to be a tortoise or a snail. Crawl slowly along the ground, acting the part yourself for them to copy.

On other occasions, you may want your children to be more active so that they get tired in time for bed later, so put on a disco for them to dance to or chase them, clapping your hands together and, when you catch them, tickle them to get them excited. If you don't actually want to run after them, act as if you are slowly turning into a monster – bring your shoulders up to your head, open your mouth and thrust your jaw out, clamp your upper arms against the side of your body and stick your forearms forward with claw like hands opening and shutting, then walk slowly towards your child, rocking from side to side on stiff legs; they will surely run!

Afterwards you can ceremoniously 'take an antidote pill' and return to normal in time to cuddle them for bed. They will love this and ask for more. You can 'be a monster' anywhere, at any time! It's free! It's fun!

However, it's not all about you and what you want as a parent. You must be sensitive to your child's needs and respond to their feedback. Pace things to suit them. If they are in a new situation and want to cling to your leg, let them take their time, don't push them away.

Beware of toddlers – they can put on an amazing burst of speed! One time I was in the garden, talking with the father of a toddling boy and before we could stop him he had fallen in the pond; his mother was not pleased with us!

KEYNOTE:

Don't forget to enlist the power of music and dance to the cause of parenting.

SANCTIONS

According to the Social Science definition, sanctions are reactions (or threats or promises of reactions) by members of a society indicating approval or disapproval of behaviour, which serve to enforce the group's standards of conduct.

Sanctions include punishments and rewards. Reward is a positive sanction, that is, the awarding of a pleasantness, whereas punishment is a negative sanction, that is, the inflicting of an unpleasantness or the deprivation of a pleasantness.

Like medications, both of these treatments have side effects. The side effect experienced by the recipient of a reward is a glowing feeling of being appreciated and integrated within the family, school or society. The side effect from a punishment is disaffection from society, a breaking of friendship bonds and a feeling of resentment and low self worth. Needless to say, reward works far better than punishment.

Please try to find every opportunity to reward your young children. Show them they can shine! Give them a kind word, a hug, a smile, sing their name and tell them they are your little lovely, or whatever your term of endearment is. There's nothing difficult or costly about it!

If they are really good, give them a small present such as a sticker, or do something for them in return such as getting them a drink. They will repay you with a desire to earn more of your approval, in other words, to be good. (This is *young* children mind you, not teenagers!)

There are all sorts of rewards that young children find acceptable. Stars, stickers, stamps, a kind word or just being the 'winner'. Find out what your child responds to and stock up on it.

You can keep a tally of good behaviour on a 'Reward Board' but, beware, rather like Diaries that you were given for Christmas, they are difficult regimes to keep going after day one! Alternatively you can keep a record of misdemeanors. Some schools use a traffic light system; every day the children start on 'green', if they do one 'naughty' they become 'yellow' and if they do two, they get a 'red'. It's a bit like the football card system. In that school, red means a note to parents; at home it could mean the withdrawal of a privilege like watching TV over dinner.

Punishment can be soft or hard: denial or withdrawal of something pleasurable is a soft punishment while the infliction of physical pain is a hard punishment. Personally, I do not recommend physical punishment. I have seen what it does to the personalities of young children. One boy was so damaged, if I raised my hand to scratch my ear he dropped to the floor cowering, mistakenly expecting my hand to come down on him, based on his past experience of men!

So, I wouldn't condone spanking. My principle is that children are people and you wouldn't spank an adult if they didn't behave. Not only that, but you wouldn't expect to be able to control the behaviour of an adult other than by persuasion. Using strength on children is merely taking advantage of their small size and is no more acceptable than it would be to use strength on an adult dwarf. The only occasions when it might be forgivable would be in cases when their safety is at risk.

Remember, if you inflict physical punishment on your children, you are legalizing brutality: *"You hit me! Why shouldn't I hit him (or you)?"* Even acrimoniously talking down to them, or 'coming down on them like a ton of bricks' as sergeant majors were famous for doing, may merely turn them against you. It is a difficult tightrope to walk.

Some of the rulers of our planet's nations have realized this – you win few friends by military force (hard power); having invaded a country you then need to ingratiate yourself with the locals by building schools, hospitals, bridges, etc. It's the same in the family – you need to exercise soft power. Recent research indicates there might be a link between harsh physical punishment of children with mood disorders, anxiety disorders, substance abuse/dependence, and personality disorders in adulthood.

http://pediatrics.aappublications.org/content/early/2012/06/27/peds.2011-2947

One researcher puts it bluntly: "Physical punishment should not be used on any child, at any age." There is not total agreement over this, however, another psychologist says, "Certainly, overly severe physical punishment is going to have adverse effects on children, but for younger kids, if spanking is used in the most appropriate way and is seen by children as motivated by concern for their behaviour and welfare, then I don't think it has a detrimental effect."

Admonition is a punishment and, therefore, is itself an aggressive act. Often, mediation works better, expressing disappointment at the behaviour of the aggressor and allowing the aggrieved child to express himself. This can enhance the understanding and, hopefully, the empathy of the aggressor. If we can make them understand, asking them whether they would like that done to them, maybe they will realise that it is not nice.

You 'orrible little oik!

You definitely will need to exercise soft punishment though; no children are so angelic that they never need punishing. The best punishment is the withdrawal of attention. Using denial of your companionship as a sanction means you have to commit time to them in order to have something to take away. You have to have a relationship with them that they enjoy so that you can deprive them of it occasionally.

First you have to give your child your attention – don't always be in your own world looking at your computer, mobile phone or tablet. Build up attention credit with them. What can you do? It's easy. Spend quality time with them. Rough and tumble play is cheap and effective – bash each other with a rolled up newspaper or throw cushions. Go for a walk and feed the ducks. Help each other to cook some scones, pancakes, muffins or cookies. Sit and watch a DVD together. Read together with your child sat on your lap. This is not rocket science!

If you have built up a track record of giving attention to your child that they have enjoyed, you can withdraw it; you can ignore your child when he or she is naughty.

There are two levels of ignoring. Passive ignoring is simply taking no notice of him or her. Unfortunately, they may not realize this is happening! Active ignoring is ostentatiously doing something else; rolling your eyes skywards and getting absorbed in your smart phone or tablet, for example.

You can even escalate to removing your presence, saying, *"I don't want to be with you if that's how you're going to behave"*. Ostracizing can be a powerful weapon against annoying behaviour. Brief parental rejection soon produces results if you have a record of having good times together.

You also can make them think of *future* outcomes by using tactics of questioning with a tacit threat such as, *"Why would I want to take a mean person swimming?" "Why would I let a mean person play on my computer?"* This lesson in the *withdrawal of deferred gratification* is a very valuable one for them to learn.

Interactions like this give a great opportunity to teach responsibility. One day my eldest daughter spilled water. I said, *"Please get the cloth and mop it up."* She did so saying, *"Why do I have to clear it up?"* I said, *"Who spilt it?"* She said, *"Me."* I said, *"Well, there you are then."* Don't let them turn you into their servant - if they mess your car up, get them to help clean their rubbish out.

If your children are really going frantic and you want things calmed down, take the oldest one aside and give them some responsibility; ask them to help getting their sibling bathed or dressed for bed. You may be surprised at the sudden change from childish to mature behaviour. That's how the British Empire was run: by indirect rule!

'Please' and *'thank you'* are expressions that lubricate social interactions. I try to insist that *'please'* comes at the start of a request, not as an afterthought tacked on the end of the sentence. That way, people are more likely to get the politeness of your intention straightaway and to react favourably. Of course you, as the parent, have to set the example by doing it yourself.

If a child shows ingratitude, one of the easiest things to do is to withdraw a service that you were, until then, willingly providing. For instance: when a child asked me, nicely, to prepare some fruit for her, I did so but, when she criticized the way I'd done it, I promptly ate the fruit myself, loudly remarking how delicious it was! Some lessons are easy to teach!

On the subject of eating, children need to be trained in table manners. At first they will keep getting up and wandering off, they will disappear under the table; they will not conform to

198

your expectations. To avoid turning this into a battleground and ruining your relationship with your children, my advice is to take them out of their comfort zone. Go to a restaurant, as soon as you think they are ready for it, or eat at friends to let them see examples of acceptable behaviour. Help them to join in and feel as though they belong by giving them 'kid's wine' (summer fruits squash)!

All children will need telling off. Even toddlers can understand a stern look and a wagging finger accompanied by the word. 'No!' We've had to do this to stop our youngest daughter clambering dangerously onto the tables. Obviously, a punishment has to be related to the 'crime' so it must occur as soon as possible after the event. If you wait until later, a child may find it difficult to associate the effect with the cause.

There are some sanctions that I would advise against making into punishments. One of them is sending a child to an early bed. Going to bed ought to be an enjoyable process of letting go of an exhausting day and drifting off to sleep. It should not be the result of a stressful incident involving being abandoned to cry behind a closed door. See more in the section 'Daily Routine'.

Obviously it is not good to deprive a child of food as a punishment, but removing treats like ice cream is fine. Another punishment I would not endorse is the taking away of toys. How is that different from theft? Weren't they a gift? Isn't a gift an irreversible transaction, unless the recipient chooses to give it back themselves? Confiscating something that is being used as a weapon is a different matter, of course.

Don't overdo it. Constantly reprimanding your child can result in the complaint, *"Nobody cares about me!"* Of course, they may just be being over dramatic. If you think that is the case, you can respond with, *"Well, have you shown other people that you care about them?"*

You really don't want to ruin their self-esteem though. When he was feeling unwanted and unloved at about six years old, one poor boy that I knew said, *"I wish I was dead!"* How would that make you feel as a parent?

If this does happen to you, it's time to assure them that you still love *them;* it's just that particular *behaviour* that you don't like. Also, don't bear a grudge. Follow up the naughty behaviour as quickly as possible with a telling-off and then let it be finished.

You may have gathered that I believe the only good form of discipline is *self-discipline*. We must help our children to discover their own discipline rather than trying to impose our discipline upon them. The old techniques of spanking, time-out, threatening (with 'Hell' or the police), withdrawing personal belongings, isolation, enforced unpleasant activities and public embarrassment are really control tactics and punishments that are not helpful in encouraging the development of self discipline and may alienate parent from child.

So what *should* you do? Calmly spend time with them – *time in*, not time out. Talk to them about what they have done, ask them how they feel and how they think others might feel. Ask them whether it was acceptable and what might have been preferable. Get them to suggest what TO DO rather than telling them what not to do.

KEYPOINT:

Reward is far better than punishment.

WHERE'S MY LOVELY TODDLER GONE?

Toddlers are a special delight! While they can't speak, you can read their body language and, later, their gestures. Today I gave my sixteen-month-old daughter half a plain digestive biscuit. She looked at one side, turned it over and looked at the other side. You could see her thinking, *"Where's the chocolate?"* She didn't need to be able to speak!

One thing you can be sure of when you are parenting is: your child will explore boundaries. Sometimes it's as early as two years old – the 'terrible twos', and sometimes it's later, but it will happen! After three delightful years with my eldest daughter, now that she is four, she is showing her wicked side!

The other day we were parked at a nature reserve in France, eating ice creams and, since it was hot and sunny, I opened the car doors to let some cool air in. Well, that was it! She screamed, cried tears and kicked the dashboard! When I was able to get sense out of her it seemed she didn't want the doors open because flies might come in! There was a convertible parked next to us with the hood down; they weren't worried about flies!

OK, she could have the doors shut but she couldn't have me. I got out and sat at a picnic table leaving her to stew in her own juice. Later, I went back and thumbed my nose at her through the window; that raised a smile.

Crotchety crying often has underlying causes and is just initiated by some unrelated event. When we drove off, we talked about her weird behaviour and I asked her if she thought I deserved an apology; she said, *"Sorry."* She was tired and trying to come to terms with some bad family news while struggling to give up her dummy (comforter), so I forgave her.

That afternoon, we had a rest on the bed together and when she woke up I showed her lots of digital photos of her as a smiling infant. She said, incongruously for a four year old, *"I loved being young!"* I said, *"Where's my lovely baby gone?"* The loss of that stage of our relationship made my eyes moist and she wiped away my tears.

Children are often affected by something other than what an adult may imagine is the issue. That same daughter suddenly announced that she didn't want hot meals at school. Knowing that the meals are very good and she has been eating them 'all up', I wondered what the real reason was. Asking her a few judicious questions soon elucidated the truth; *"Do you sit with your friends for hot meals?"* Guess what? Her friends take a packed lunch!

As they grow up, our children alter the social dynamic in our homes. The mood changes from one of joy, influenced by the antics of a cute toddler, to increasing grumpiness as the reality of daily school attendance hits them and culminating in the obstreperous teenager. We have to guard against turning domestic bliss into a war zone as lines of demarcation appear, 'sides' are taken and a tussle for supremacy between kids and parents breaks out.

205

KEYPOINT:

Children change as they grow and develop, not only in size but also in personality.

SCHOOL

A milestone in life! After years, rather too many because of her birth date, happily going to pre-school, my eldest daughter has started 'Big School'. She's been ready for it for ages since her peer group all went up last year leaving her with the babies. I took her on an exciting three months long holiday to New Zealand and weekend trips around the UK to expand her experience and give variety to her life. The pre-school was marvelous, it was just that she was the tallest and most mature by far; she beat the boys in all the races with her long legs!

She was so ready for 'big' school that she persuaded me to buy a uniform dress six months before she needed it and regularly dressed up in it, even going to pre-school wearing it! So you can imagine we had a count down towards the start of term at the Infant school.

Now, at the end of the second full week, we have had the first morning of, *"I don't want to go to school!"* It's understandable – the excitement of newness has worn off and we had such fun playing with her eighteen-month-old sister throughout the summer holiday that she wants to go back to that regime.

We got over it by saying she could choose her morning snack and going to the local shop to buy it. It's her birthday party in a couple of weeks so we can change the subject and talk about what present she wants, where we should hold her party and who to invite.

It's always difficult coping with change but the best method for handling it is in a non-confrontational way. If you have a younger one you can pass some responsibility to the new school child by suggesting he/she could set an example; they sometimes respond to that.

Hopefully they will settle into the routine soon enough and then you will only have to distinguish between occasions when they are genuinely ill or faking a 'sicky'!

WHY DON'T YOU DO AS YOU'RE TOLD?
(The Folly of Telling)

How many mums and dads have voiced this plea? What about yourself, dear reader? Did you always do as you were told when you were a child? How about now you're an adult? What do you do when you see the sign, WET PAINT? You touch it to check, don't you! Do you often find yourself coming up against people who don't do exactly as they're told? I think you'll find it's very common! A better question would be, *"Why do we still expect our children to do as they're told?"*

This is a good time to bring back Confucious' saying, *'I hear and I forget, I see and I remember, I do and I understand'.* Our ears are the sensory organs that are given less attention by the brain (except by the blind) so don't expect to get a great response if this is the only route you are using for communication!

This may be a counter-intuitive behaviour management technique, but my advice is: *try not to instruct.* Instead, phrase communications as questions or requests. Instead of saying, *"Don't do that!"* try, *"How would you like that to be done to you?"* or *"What might happen if you do that?"* Get them to think, and instead of *"Do this"* try *"Please would you do this for me?"* or, *"Would you like to help?"* You can even attempt the blatant, *"If I asked you nicely, would you…"*

My advice is always try to avoid telling. Asking questions such as, *"Can you think of another way of doing that?"* is less likely to be considered patronizing and will give an opportunity for the recipient to invent the solution and feel good about themselves. If you treat your children with respect, ask their opinions, consult them on decisions and generally behave democratically towards them, as if you are dealing with little adults, they will respond in kind, hopefully.

Of course, there will be some occasions when it *is* necessary to say 'don't' such as, *"Don't throw sand, it can hurt your eyes."* However, overdoing it will just devalue it, so use it sparingly!

Now I'm going to go against my own advice with a string of 'Don'ts'! Don't make your household into a monument to the ineffectiveness of *telling* as a strategy for behaviour management. Do you want your children to continually need to be corrected, to copy that tactic themselves, to bossily correct each other and even to cheekily correct you? If you do, then set them the example that human interaction is all about correcting; it's an easy impression to convey!

Assuming you don't want that, avoid over correction: humans are apes and we learn by aping. Don't teach your children conflict. When you realize you are about to start a sentence with the word 'Don't', bite your tongue!

If you've never told your child off, when you do it for the first time it has an amazing effect. It stopped my two-year-old daughter in her tracks! Don't keep telling off - the more you do it the less effective it becomes. Did the prisoners of war in Colditz castle meekly succumb to the regime of the German guards? No! They were stimulated to rebel against the rule-bound authority and plot to escape. They were not naughty men; they were expressing human nature.

Avoid the Battle of Wills or your children will come to expect conflict and consider it to be normal human interaction. They will develop challenging behaviour. They will come to disagree with everything you say just as a matter of course. In school this may manifest itself as 'barrack room lawyer syndrome' and their reports may describe them as 'astute' – a teacher euphemism for cunning, sly or crafty. You may feel you have to react by saying, *"Don't do that"* and, *"Do this"* even more often! Your home will become a war zone! Do you want disagreeable children?

If you do get into a conflict, let them see you consult

someone else for advice. For example, if your daughter is demanding sandals, ask a shop assistant what shoes they would choose to wear on a rainy day like today. It's part of the 'it takes a village to raise a child' mentality, disengage yourself from the warzone – let them hear another's opinion. So much historical baggage develops between children and parents that disagreements can get to be more about the participants than the issues.

KEYPOINT:

To reduce conflict, adopt a policy of low intervention. Bossiness is counter-productive. Relax. Remember, *telling* simply doesn't work! Release your control a little! Make the company of members of your family something to mutually enjoy!

PETS

Pets are like little people who can't speak, silently beseeching you to care for them! They are beneficial to the raising of children in at least two respects. They give children an opportunity to care for a living creature, which is great for developing empathy; some children develop their first 'true love' for a pet. Pets also give a child experience of the mechanics of life – feeding, drinking, excreting, reproducing, getting ill and, eventually, dying.

Some pets, particularly dogs, are great for showing children the process of training – it's good for them to see how another animal is taught to fit into the family home and human society in general. It is especially good for them to see a dog being disciplined when it is naughty; it helps them to understand that there are barriers to acceptable behaviour.

If you can accommodate a pet for your growing child, I would recommend that you should. So what sort of pet should you get?

CAGED MAMMALS AND BIRDS

Mice, rats, and hamsters can be great fun and are relatively painless to keep. They will fit into even the smallest of flats or apartments without suffering. Hamsters, mice and rats have a life expectancy of just a couple of years so grief will come soon. Don't think of pet rats as nasty disease-carrying wild rodents; the domesticated ones are very clean, cute and friendly and you can have a relationship with them more than with mice and hamsters.

Guinea pigs and rabbits consume more food and need more space than the smaller mammals. They should really be kept outside with a fox proof house and run. You can bring them in to play when the weather is foul but don't expect to be able to house train them. A warning, it's difficult to tell males from females with these animals when they are newly born; they become sexually mature at three weeks and they are not averse to copulating with their siblings! Since a litter can number up to eight, you have to have plenty of cages ready to separate males from females or you will see lots of birth defects due to inbreeding. This is what is meant by, 'breeding like rabbits'! I wouldn't recommend breeding them unless you are going into the business.

"Breeding like rabbits"

Budgies are great. They are less popular now than when I was a boy, probably because it is fashionable to consider caging a bird as unethical. If you let them out for a while everyday (be sure to shut the windows and doors!) they will get plenty of exercise walking and flying round your room. They are intelligent and loving if you get them just a few weeks old when they will imprint on you as part of their family in the same way that the goslings imprinted upon early

215

behaviourist, Konrad Lorenz. You can handle them (very gently!) and they can form strong bonds with their owners. With a lifespan of about ten years they are more of a commitment than a mouse or hamster.

Many temperate birds have a nice character too but they do sloppy poo, unlike the tropical ones. I had a pet starling for a while and had to have a 'starling pullover' especially to receive the poo when it sat on my shoulder. Once you have raised a fledgling it is practically impossible to release them because they have not learned the skills of a wild bird, so I wouldn't recommend adopting a baby bird from nature.

CATS AND DOGS

Cats are easy pets. They are friendly but independent. They are clean in their own territory, they do not require walking because they come and go through a cat flap, but they sometimes invite their friends back to their home! They do not form strong bonds but will allow themselves to be petted. You can't train them to do tricks and the only sort of play they are interested in is one that mimics chasing prey. You may get your furniture scratched when they sharpen their claws and they may bring you presents of their latest kill. It has been said that dogs have owners but cats have staff!

Dogs are demanding but rewarding. Not called 'man's best friend' for nothing, you can have an understanding with a dog more than with any other pet. It works both ways; in recent research using eighteen different breeds of dogs, fifteen of them showed 'person-oriented behaviour' when they encountered a person (not necessarily their owner) who was crying. They respond to the emotional tone of our voices and some of them are chauvinists who may be more obedient to men than to women!

Since they are pack animals, they do not like being on their own. I have witnessed some very cruel treatment of dogs by ignorant owners. One couple left their Alsatian locked in their garage while they went out to work all day. The poor animal barked its distress constantly and probably became psychotic.

Dogs come in different sizes; the bigger they are the more food and exercise they need and the more havoc they are capable of causing. Bigger dogs have bigger teeth to chew your furniture with, more drool, more gas in their farts and bigger poos, which need to be picked up and disposed of nowadays. Pets do funny things; have you seen a dog suddenly get up and move away? He has probably just done a fart too smelly even for himself!

I was lucky, I had three Labradors, one after another, during my early life although it was a more dog-friendly society then – we didn't have to pick up their poo! Perhaps people should consider not having a dog unless they have a very big garden and one adult always at home (my mother was our home-maker back then), or some other way of providing the environment these animals require.

Whatever pet you have should be provided with a rich and stimulating environment and lots of interaction or, just like humans, they may become depressed. This condition may manifest itself in the animal's posture and appearance – tail down, mangy coat or shabby feathers.

KEYPOINT:

Pets are important in a child's life. They let them learn about caring and they repay them with devotion. These are priceless lessons.

> *"If I wanted a friend, I'd get a dog!"*
>
> Lord Sugar
> in 'The Apprentice'

TOYS AND GAMES

Children do not need expensive toys! The box a toy comes in is often more fun than the toy itself! Why not scrounge some big empty boxes from your local shops? Boxes can become houses, boats, seats, tables – your children will use their imagination. Let them make a 'den' with a sheet hanging over a table. You can make a balloon out of the plastic bag the bread or the magazine came in! Great fun can be had with a real balloon playing keepy-uppy; when you have a helium-filled party balloon you can try keepy-downy, that's hilarious fun as long as you do it in a room with a low ceiling!

You can flick an elastic band off your thumb for your child to fetch or fire back at you. Learn how to make paper planes. An old envelope can become a monster! Toddlers love tearing up paper – give them the junk mail! Visit Facebook group totstoteens to see videos of fun activities.

At the risk of sounding like a fogey, I'm going to tell you that I genuinely didn't have much more than a stick to play with as a boy. I know you're not going to believe me, and you're going to think that I must have been outside kicking a ball like you did. Well, no! There were hardly any balls in post-war England.

Plastic technology had not yet reached the stage of development necessary for ball production. At that time, footballs were hand sewn from leather with an inflatable rubber bladder inside. Cricket balls are *still* made in the old traditional way using cork and leather. Back then, we had a few discarded tennis balls, and that was it, apart from some golf balls, but what could you do with them? The main point is: footballs were too expensive for us to own. Schools could afford a stock, but wisely kept them under lock and key.

We were allowed penknives, so outside activities included cutting sticks from the bushes to make bows and arrows or for damming the local stream. We built camouflaged camps from branches or piled up great fortifications of grass mowings and charged at each other in war games. We riskily investigated the tunnels leading to the empty petrol tanks of the bombed fuel station at the bottom of the road.

There was early cyclocross: races against the clock around a rough course through the woods sharing our one bike and the only wristwatch that had a second hand. I broke my nose doing that. This variety of play developed our creativity and skills. When we were a bit older, we made gunpowder from materials that were easily available in those days!

If anyone did manage to get hold of a ball he could guarantee that he would have something else: friends! A ball gave you power. You immediately became captain and could select your team. If you didn't win, you could take the ball away in a huff! Or you could lend it to a chum knowing that he would feel really privileged because he understood the significance of your sacrifice. Then it got a puncture and the fun was over for weeks until another one appeared, maybe as someone's birthday present.

Because they were really rare when I was a boy, we couldn't spend much time playing with balls. Instead, we collected tea cards, constructed model aircraft from balsa wood and tissue paper or we borrowed books from the library. Girls made daisy chains and learned knitting and sewing. Hardly anyone complained of being bored; we were used to making up our own activities and did not expect to be entertained.

No one with a brain should ever be bored, merely unchallenged! So invent a challenge: how would you find out the amount of rain falling? Can you make a shaker from a plastic bottle and some beans? I bet you can't work out the number of blades of grass in the lawn!

So, almost anything can become a toy. Let your child play with water in the sink or bath, finding out about pouring, floating and sinking. We have a double sink so we can sit a small child in an empty one and let them safely play in the, water filled, other one. Later, you can add some washing up liquid or ice to revive interest. If you can stand the noise, allow them to bash your saucepans!

When you're in a car, go, "Errrrrrrmmmm" in a slowly rising pitch as you go up a hill and, "Weeeee!" as you come down the other side. From the age of one to about three years they will love this and will join in!

Last week we went to a theme park. We arrived before it was open and met another early family. Our excited children played chase around the advert column and tried to catch drops of rain from the leaky gutter of the ticket office in their mouths! We had so much fun we could have saved the entry cost and gone home! Who needs toys?

Play with them yourself; this doesn't require any props. A parent can have lots of bubbly fun with a child in the bath. If they resist getting into a bath make it more fun with a new sponge or toy, and tell them they don't want to be smelly! In other rooms, you can pick them up and throw them into the air (be careful, they need never leave your hands to become briefly weightless) or hold them under the arms and spin them round. Take them to the local playground or swimming

224

pool. Bash them with the vacuum formed plastic box the cakes come in! Throw rolled up balls of paper at them! They will appreciate those things more than anything – it's your attention they are getting!

You've got hands, haven't you? There are so many ways to amuse a young child with a hand! Use two fingers to 'walk' towards them going *'dum, dum, dum, dum'* with every step then *'diddly, diddly, diddly'* as you reach the target and tickle! Use all four fingers to 'walk' and you've got a spider for them to run away from! Show your child how to make silhouettes on the wall using a table lamp. Do a dog and make his mouth open and shut and his ear wiggle. Do a baby crocodile and grab your child's finger in its 'mouth'.

Can you make a farting sound with your hands? What about a big click using both hands? Blindman's buff only requires a tea towel folded diagonally and tied round a child's head – teach them to stick their hands out in front as they move forward.

How about playing 'Olympics'? Just set a task like running from the sitting room to the kitchen and time them. Let them try to beat their record and then get them to stand on a stool for the presentation. Hum the national anthem while you award their gold medal and then interview them, *"How does it feel to be on the podium as a winner?"*

Ok, you are going to have to buy scooters and bicycles when the time comes but by then I hope you will have started giving your child some pocket money so they have begun to understand value.

The one thing I'm going to recommend that you buy for your child as soon as you can afford it is a tablet computer. My daughters were able to negotiate their way around the intuitive touch sensitive screen of a smart phone from the age of about one and a half. The educational apps and games are invaluable learning aids and the children's videos and access to the CBeebies website, etc. provide great opportunities for introducing language and concepts of modern life. You can take a tablet computer with you in a car, a hotel, to foreign country; how ever did we manage before?
A warning, don't make a household computer the property of a child by giving it to them as a present. You will give them the power to deny others the use of it. You wouldn't give them the oven or the washing machine would you?

KEYPOINT:

Pleasure from play need not be costly!

226

RELIGION

Imagine:

"You are newly born. Your eyes don't focus properly yet. You are programmed to be cute so your parents will fall in love with you and look after you while you are helpless. You gurgle and cry and soon learn to lock eyes with your carers and to smile fetchingly. You have no hatred. You have no religion.

If your parents happen to be Christian, they are about to fill you up with Christianity. If they are Muslim, you will get a dose of Islam. Jewish: Judaism, Hindu: Hinduism, Buddhist: Buddhism. Dear reader, I think you get the picture.

In some cases, your parents will have pieces cut off your genitalia. They, and their priests, will teach you that the religion you have been dedicated to without consultation, after all you can't speak yet, is the only right one and all other beliefs are wrong.

You may be sent to a single faith school, which will confirm the impression that your religion makes you special and divides you from the rest of society. A few of your peers may become radicalized into fundamentalists and may kill 'in

God's name'."

KEYPOINT:

Repeated exposure to rituals in the early period of life results in difficulty escaping from a doctrine at a later stage.

Please raise your children in a secular way. If they want to join a religion when they are old enough to make an informed decision, that's up to them.

ILLNESS AND INJURY

Young children spread diseases like nobody's business! They put everything in their mouths and sneeze and dribble over everyone else! It's nature's way of challenging their immune systems and arming them with immunity for later in life. When they go to school they will be in an ideal environment for contagion and infection. They will bring home illnesses and infect you! Our youngest has a cute habit of putting her fingers into our mouths just to make sure of an effective transfer of pathogens!

How do you tell if your toddler is ill? Well, before they can speak you only have signs and symptoms to go on. Sick children can be grumpier than usual, they often cry for apparently no reason and tantrums break out. You will become an expert at feeling their temperature with your hand on their forehead – a hand can develop into quite a sensitive thermometer! If they are slightly hot, the first thing to try is an appropriate dose of children's analgesic such as 'Calpol', which may help them cool down and take a healing nap.

You can expect your child to get 'nits' (head lice) and many colds when they start mixing with other children. Chicken pox is best got over in childhood and usually confers lifelong immunity. I didn't get it until I was forty; it was not a pleasant experience!

Recent research indicates that many residents of Glasgow have inherited unusually active immune systems thanks to their ancestors being raised cheek by jowl in crowded tenements where they were exposed to an unusually high level of infection. Unfortunately, in today's more hygienic world their immune systems, now less challenged, do what overactive immune systems do; they turn on their own bodies. Glaswegians tend to experience more autoimmune conditions, such as rheumatoid arthritis, at an earlier stage of life than the rest of the UK, and to have a lower life expectancy.

No parent wants their children to get badly ill so we all need to be on the watch to catch things early. The Internet is a great help nowadays with masses of information available. Children respond quickly to infection with a raised temperature and often appear well during the day only for the temperature to go up at bedtime. Keep a thermometer handy – you can now get inexpensive ear thermometers like the professionals use in hospitals. A higher than normal temperature is nature's way of combating disease; it may be unpleasant for us, but the bugs (pathogens) must hate it even more because it kills them!

Having a smaller body (greater surface to volume ratio) means very young children are much more sensitive to external temperature changes than adults. I have had experience of two babies who become overheated (hyperthermia). They were taken out, well wrapped up, on cold days and then brought home in warm cars. Their bodies over-heated and they started to fit, which is alarming. The solution is to cool them down by stripping off all their clothing and fanning them or applying wet cloths to their bare skin. Always call an ambulance if in doubt.

Watch out for meningitis, a potentially life-threatening disease, which has flu like symptoms initially, see:

http://www.nhs.uk/conditions/meningitis/pages/symptoms.aspx

Do have your children vaccinated. Don't fall for the scaremongering press releases, which link MMR vaccine with autism. There is no evidence to support this and, thanks to ill-advised mums denying their children protection and spoiling the 'herd immunity', two children have needlessly died from measles in the UK. Andrew Wakefield, the Doctor who irresponsibly started this rumour, has been deregistered. Thanks to the increased level of public skepticism to vaccination that he initiated, there has been a resurgence of whooping cough in the UK.

Minor illnesses can be treated with infant paracetamol and minor injuries with plasters. Lessons can be taught when injuries occur – *"Play safely, always keep the plasters in the same place!"* etc. Hurt children need comforting; 'kissing it better' or 'magic water' works well for a few years then you need to start encouraging bravery with something like, *"Look, you will have a fabulous scar from this! You will be able to show your war wounds and brag about how you survived!"*

Some children discover that being hurt is rewarded by increased parental attention, cuddles, etc. Cunningly, they then adopt a policy of coming out in sympathy with whatever is the disease of the moment! When they are very young you might like to play along with them and give them a pretend plaster, but later it's necessary to point it out when there is no blood!

KEYPOINT:

Always call in the experts if you are uncertain about what to do – there is plenty of help available on the internet and telephone.

RISK

In the last few decades we have become very risk conscious. Strategies are changed in response to the analysis of statistics and the Health and Safety Executive is in charge of monitoring and reducing the UK's accidents rate.

This has had an effect on Science teaching. Many years ago, I used to demonstrate the lightness of hydrogen by blowing football-sized bubbles of town gas (not pure hydrogen nor natural gas) and releasing them to float up to the ceiling. I'd get the naughtiest boy to stand on the bench and light them with a flaming taper on the way up! A ring of fire would leave a scorch mark on the ceiling! That boy would be my friend for life and I would be the class's favourite teacher!

Today I'd have to fill in a risk assessment form and, in the remote chance of anything happening, my neck would be on the block. This has discouraged many exciting experiments and Science has become a more boring subject. Instead we have to explain the dangers of things. It's far better to *show* them the dangers. Explaining won't work – remember we don't like being told – so let them see it happen!

I suspect that focusing on warnings will never work for the more adventurous person, especially when they become know-all teenagers. Some of the terrible accidents due to throwing accelerants such as petrol (gasoline) on to barbecues undoubtedly result from the person's ignorance of the chemicals being used and overconfidence in his ability to control fire. I even know a chemistry teacher who got his hands badly burned in this way! He is no advert for his profession! Maybe the best way we can prevent this type of accident is not by telling but by *showing*.

When I was a young boy, our family home was kept warm in winter by coal fires. Sometimes it was difficult to get them lit. My father used to hold a page of a broadsheet newspaper (using his hands and his knees to press it against the fire surround) covering the fireplace opening just leaving a hole at the bottom so air could get in under the grate. This set up a draught route through the hot kindling and a blaze soon resulted. If the paper caught fire, as it frequently did, we simply screwed it up and tossed it onto the fire!

I recommend giving your child experience of fire. Using candles and matches, for example, will foster understanding rather than ignorance. Show them; allow them to have a go. Let them see how risky things are and they will act with due caution. The same is true of other things – you can easily show them that spiders are harmless, for example, by handling them yourself.

KEYPOINT:

Show your children the harmfulness of dangerous things and the harmlessness of safe things.

INFLUENCES

There are many different forms of media capable of exerting influences these days: DVDs, hundreds of TV channels, Youtube, Social Media, MP3s, radio, magazines, computer games, etc. The question is, 'Are children influenced by what they see or hear?'

Of course they are! In my young day there was Saturday morning kids' cinema; we saw a black and white film about 'Tobor' the robot. Tobor went rogue and chased the humans (very slowly)! We came out of that cinema and walked stiff legged with our arms bent forward from the elbow. I did the most frightening impression so all my friends ran away from me in mock terror.

The Lone Ranger was serialized for the Saturday Kids' Cinema so our favourite game was Cowboys and Indians. We rampaged through the local woodland making shooting noises with our mouths and gun shapes with our hands. Cops and Robbers never caught on to the same extent.

When I started teaching, in a boys' school, the pupils did play fighting during breaks and, just as we had when I was their age, there were unwritten rules. Punching and wrestling was ok, but kicking, pinching and biting were considered 'dirty'. Then Bruce Lee's film 'Enter the Dragon' came out. The very next week, the boys started kicking each other! Martial arts had arrived in the UK.

Later, working in a co-ed comprehensive, it became essential for staff to watch the children's TV series, 'Grange Hill', because our pupils would try out on us the tricks that they had seen done in the fictional school the night before! The teachers who hadn't seen the episode fell for the tricks; forewarned is forearmed!

A couple of years ago when I was teaching AS level Biology, a girl said to me, *"I have no idea what you just said."* I was slightly annoyed thinking, *"You're trying to make it my fault!"* I have recently discovered that she was just trying out a line from the internet – it's a 'meme' you can have on your T-shirt!

Nowadays, I can see my four-year-old daughter copying the behaviour of CBBC's Tracey Beaker. I notice her trying out parts of the script on me, *"I hate you! There is nothing I like about you!"* Doesn't that form of words just reveal the dead hand of a scriptwriter? I never use the word 'hate' so she has probably picked it up from there. She sometimes gives a clue that she is pretending by calling me 'Teacher'! Don't tell me the media has no influence on society! If it doesn't, what is the advertising business doing?

Does media influence make children into bad persons? No! Normal kids learn to distinguish acting from real life. But sadly, a few with psychopathic tendencies will become fixated on 'snuff' videos or other antisocial material and act out their fantasies on other members of society. Several crazy gunmen have been found to have collections of shootout videos and pedophiles' computer memories are usually riddled with child pornography.

Maybe the influences do not create the rotten behaviour, perhaps they merely encourage an existing predisposition. I suspect that some of the early home experiences like the events witnessed by the children at that Special Needs School where I taught for a while may have predisposed them.

Let's hope we can guide our own children down the right path with our example and advice.

CONCLUSION

Please note, this is a book not a stone tablet! I'm not preaching a doctrine! I'm still learning myself!

We all have our own individual style of parenting and the vast majority of us manage to make a decent fist of it. How will you know you are succeeding? Well, your children will compete to sit on your lap! They will prefer your company to others. They will do what you ask more willingly than they will obey others, but, however you bring up your children, there is one thing you can be sure of: they will be delightful and infuriating in roughly equal measure!

Just this year I found out the truth about a memorable event in my boys' childhood; one evening we heard a crash followed by crying. We went to investigate and found my eldest son on the floor having fallen out of the top bunk. He had landed on his cricket bat, which he'd left on the floor and was quite hurt. How could that have happened? Well, my younger son, now thirty-five years old, recently confessed that they had both been in the top bunk fighting and he had pushed his brother out! He had got in the bottom bunk as he heard his parents approached and tried to look innocent! They had kept it secret from their parents; I might have died never knowing!

You know the car sticker that says, 'A puppy is not just for Christmas'? Well, just think how much more true that message is when you apply it to your pet humans! Dogs may live for a decade or even two but, hopefully, your children will outlive their parents and, although they should eventually fly the nest, they will remain your children for all of your life.

This book has focused on the early years and the accompanying website offers you the opportunity to join in with your own contributions. Please visit www.totstoteens.org.uk or Facebook group Totstoteens and upload your experiences – we would love to see pictures of the joy you have with your young children, to hear your anecdotes and suggestions, including warnings about what not to do!

I hope you have enjoyed this book and that you find some of the hints useful. Thank you for reading!

Enjoy Your Children!